FROM EGYPT
TO CANAAN

FROM EGYPT
TO CANAAN

John Ritchie

JOHN RITCHIE LTD
CHRISTIAN PUBLICATIONS

40 Beansburn, Kilmarnock, Scotland

ISBN 0 946351 80 5

Typeset by John Ritchie Ltd., Kilmarnock
Printed by Bell & Bain Ltd., Glasgow

Contents

Publishers' Preface

"Egypt to Canaan" is one of the books written by Mr John Ritchie about one hundred years ago, by means of which several generations of believers have been introduced to the rich pastures of Old Testament typical teaching. In the belief that such teaching is timeless in its relevance and applicability, John Ritchie Ltd has commissioned and produced this new edition in a style, format and language suited to present day readers. They are grateful to Dr. Bert Cargill for editing and revising this book to make it available in this form.

The epic journey of around two million people, slaves just freed from terrible conditions, crossing barriers of sea and desert to reach their promised land, is one of the truly great episodes of history. The skill of Moses makes him stand out as one of the greatest leaders of nations. But of course the main point is that this story is part of God's record of His dealings with men, His intervention in human history to accomplish His greater purposes of grace and government. And, as we are frequently reminded in the pages which follow, these things "written aforetime were written for our learning", so that we ought to turn to them again and again to learn about the power and grace of our God, the love and sacrifice of our Saviour, and the never failing resources available for us as we make our way across the wilderness of this present evil world. Great benefit will also be obtained by reading along with this one, John Ritchie's companion volumes entitled *Feasts of Jehovah* and *The Tabernacle in the Wilderness*.

The short chapters of this book are self-contained studies

of topics of spiritual value, as we follow the Israelites from Egypt to Canaan, from their redemption by blood to the consummation of their hopes, through trial and defeat and victory too, in everything finding out the absolute dependability of their God in spite of the fickleness of their own hearts. Here therefore is instruction for us, for are not the stories of our lives like that also?

February 1999
John Ritchie Ltd
Kilmarnock

CHAPTER 1

Types in the Bible

In the Bible, God has employed a variety of methods to teach us about Himself and His ways. Some of its sixty six books are historical records, others are beautiful poetry, others personal letters, and others accurate prophecies, all written by human authors inspired directly by the Holy Spirit of God. Within these books we find parables, metaphors, illustrations and types, from which God will teach us important spiritual lessons if we are willing to learn them. The subject matter of Holy Scripture transcends the limits of our natural minds, for it deals with the eternal and infinite. But God wishes to transmit His truth to us and He does so in a way that we can grasp, by writing in His Book of things we can relate to in everyday life, then leading us from these into deeper thoughts about spiritual and eternal matters.

In the Old Testament, a special method of teaching for us is in the types. In the book of Hebrews they are called patterns (9:23), figures (9:24), and shadows (10:1). This means that events and things described in the Old Testament are there to help us to understand the spiritual truths of the New Testament and apply them to ourselves. So when we use the word *type* in reference to the Old Testament we take it to mean a representation or symbol of some aspect of New Testament teaching which was then in the future, but now, for us, has been revealed in all its fullness. A study of the type assists our grasp of the truth and often highlights its detail and its beauty. The truth is so important that we need all the help we can get to understand it better and to encourage us to apply it to our lives.

Along the margin of a well-read Bible, its owner had once written this simple but true testimony to the value of Old Testament teaching:

> *"In the Old Testament the New lies hidden;*
> *In the New Testament the Old lies open".*

Put another way this could read,

> *"The New is in the Old concealed;*
> *The Old is in the New revealed".*

Many people consider that the books of the Old Testament were useful for times of long ago, but are not of much value to us at the present time. But this cannot be right. Those who carelessly pass over these parts of Holy Scripture, cannot do so without losing much that would be of great value to their souls. Remember "All Scripture is given by inspiration of God and is *profitable* for doctrine, for reproof, for correction, for instruction in righteousness" (2 Tim 3:16); and "Whatsoever things were written aforetime were written for our learning, that we through patience and comfort of the Scriptures might have hope" (Rom 15:4). These verses assure us that *all* parts of the Bible are the breathings of God, His inspired Word, and that they are indeed of practical value to us today. The books of Genesis, Exodus, Leviticus, Numbers, and Deuteronomy, are full of teaching which points to Christ. To the christian reader they are full of rich interest, for they speak of Him in whom "dwelleth all the fulness of the Godhead bodily" (Col 2:9).

These books may be compared to a great picture gallery, in which the Christ of the New Testament is seen, in all the varied glories of His person and work. Christ is the key to all these parts of Holy Scripture. There we can read about Him in type or picture form, for everything was pointing forward to Him. When *He* is known and loved, when His blessed person is the centre of our affections, it will not be hard to recognise Him, even although in some of the types we read about, He is hidden.

It has been said, "Love is quick sighted," and love can see

beauties where others fail to find them. This is true regarding heavenly things. Love to Jesus, and true heart longings after Him, are the best qualifications for seeing Christ in the Old Testament and understanding the typical scriptures, as we usually call these books. No single type could have told out all His worth, therefore there are many of them, and even then the "half hath not been told". To know all that Jesus is, the depth of His love and the glory of His person, is for a future day. What we do not know now, we shall know then, when we see Him as He is. Meanwhile we need to have our understandings opened, and our hearts stirred and engaged with Him. May He who journeyed with the two on the road to Emmaus, expound to us also the things concerning Himself in all these Scriptures (Luke 24:27).

When we see the Lord Jesus in these types, we shall see ourselves also, for we are one with Him. Some of the types, therefore, speak of the believer's union with Christ: of salvation as well as the Saviour; deliverance as well as the Deliverer; those who are being led home to heaven as well as Him who is taking us there.

Of course we realise that in the New Testament we now have a brighter light and a clearer testimony, for the Lord Jesus has been here Himself in this world. The only begotten Son from "the bosom of the Father" has been on earth, and we can trace His footsteps through the pages of the four Gospels, from Bethlehem to Calvary, and back again to heaven. Divine love has now been fully revealed, and divine justice has been wholly satisfied at the cross of Christ - things that no type could really express properly and completely. The cross alone bears full testimony that "God is light" and "God is love".

An old writer has said that in the types "God was taking His Christ and showing Him to us in parts". They speak to us of one Christ, but in His varied glories. Take, for example, the sacrifices and offerings described in Leviticus. They show the one sacrifice and offering of Jesus Christ, but in its many aspects, as burnt-offering, meat-offering, peace-offering, sin-offering, and trespass-offering. It is the same in the other types. Each in its own measure shows the worth and beauty of the Lord Jesus.

It was from one of these typical books (Numbers) that the blessed Master taught Nicodemus the story of His own death (John 3:14), how He would be lifted up on the cross. This is what we would call the *antitype* of the serpent lifted up on the pole. From another book (Deuteronomy) He chose the words by which He defeated the devil in the wilderness (Luke 4:4-12). In 1 Corinthians 10:11, we have the divine warrant for regarding the history of Israel as a type of our own: "All these things happened unto them for ensamples (the Greek word is *tupos*, from which we get our word *types),* and they are written for our admonition upon whom the ends of the world are come."

Believers have always found much to encourage and edify them in these scriptures. Young believers should be often drawn to them, for they describe so well their own case, and tell the story of what goes on in the kingdom of God within their own souls. Whether it be our trials or triumphs, failures or successes, joys or sorrows, ups or downs, all are represented in the Old Testament histories.

In the following short chapters we are going to look at some of the early and eventful history of the nation of Israel as recorded in the books of Exodus, Numbers, and Joshua. We will follow their journey from Egypt to Canaan, for it is a wonderful story. Unlike many human biographies, it shows us the dark side as well as the bright side, it tells the blunders as well as the victories of this redeemed people. It shows what the Christian's path often is, as well as what it ought to be. These pages will help you in the study of the Word of God, and help you in your own journey through life, as you take your Bible and read it prayerfully along with each chapter as we proceed.

CHAPTER 2

Egypt - the Wilderness - Canaan

The Scriptures show us three different places or positions of the children of Israel at this point in their history. Each of them is typical of our present place and position as believers in Christ. You should be able to recognise yourself in each one of them.

1. Israel in Egypt

Here they are sheltered by the blood which has been applied to the lintel of the door (Exod 12:1-13). They are safe and secure from judgement, and at peace with God. In their houses, feasting on the roast lamb, their loins are girded, their shoes are on their feet and a staff is in their hand. They are calmly waiting and ready to depart from Egypt altogether, where death and judgement are about to take place.

This shows the Christian living in a condemned world, sheltered by the blood of Christ, and delivered from wrath to come. In the midst of death he is in life, and for him judgement is past. The blood of the Lamb of God is the answer to all the claims of justice. In the enjoyment of peace with God, he is feasting on the lamb that was slain, type of a suffering Christ. Wearing pilgrim's clothing, he stands on the tip-toe of expectation, waiting for the hour when the Lord shall call him from earth to heaven. Meanwhile, he is in the world, but not of it. The blood on the lintel is between him and the Egyptians outside, and he has been commanded not to leave his separated position until the morning (Exod 12:22).

In Egypt, the Israelite is sheltered, feasting, and waiting.

Similarly, in the world today, the believer has salvation in Christ, communion with Christ, and hope of a returning Christ, as in 1 Thessalonians 1:9-10.

2. Israel in the Wilderness

Separated to God, the Red Sea which they crossed (Exodus 14) has now become a barrier between them and Egypt, separating them from the scenes of their slavery and idolatry for ever. They are a chosen people, dwelling alone, not reckoned among the nations (Num 23:9). God is their guide, for the pillar of cloud hovers above them to lead the way. They are going to be fed by God's manna daily falling from heaven; they will drink of His water flowing from the smitten rock; they will walk in His light, and fight under His banner. Egypt is *behind* them, Canaan *before* them, and God is *with* them.

This shows the believer, delivered from this present evil world by the cross of Christ (Gal 1:4); crucified to the world (Gal 6:14), dead and buried with Christ (Col 2:12), a stranger in a strange land (1 Pet 2:11), and looking forward to a better, even a heavenly country (Heb 11:16).

Like a pilgrim, he walks quietly along the King's highway, rendering to Caesar the things that are Caesar's, and to God the things that are God's, taking nothing to do with the government of the nations around him. His Father's eye is over him, and he walks looking up. All his resources are in God, depending on Him for the daily supply of every need. It is a walk of faith, consequently of trial and often of failure. Here it is that the bitter waters of Marah are tasted, immediately followed by the sweet waters and palm trees of Elim. Here Amalek comes out to fight the pilgrim; but God is *with* him now, as He had been *for* him at the Red Sea, and so his enemies are all defeated, for "God is stronger than His foes".

For the believer, the wilderness is "The School of God". There he learns experimentally his own worthlessness and weakness, and proves the grace and power of a present God. He knows now, not only in theory, but in often painful experience, that in his flesh dwells no good thing. It has had opportunity to show its true character, and has done so. Here, too, he proves the God of all grace, enough for every emergency; restoring him when he falls, strengthening him when he is weak, in battle his deliverer, in hunger his storehouse and his barn, at every stage of the way.

It is good to hear young believers singing, "I know my sins are all forgiven", and "Heaven is my home", as they take their first steps on the wilderness journey, just as Israel stood and sang their song of deliverance on the shore of the Red Sea (Exodus 15). But it is even better to see an old pilgrim leaning on his staff, with the long dreary wilderness behind him, all the lifelong discipline finished, the ups and downs, the failures and restorations past. Standing there on the *last* step of the desert, we can hear him exclaim as Caleb did, "Behold the Lord hath kept me alive as He said, these forty and five years . . . as yet I am as strong this day as I was in the day that Moses sent me, as my strength was then, even so is my strength now for war, both to go out and come in" (Josh 14:10,11). He has learned himself, and proved God; and this is a lifetime experience. Surely when we stand in His light, and look back over all the rugged road the Lord our God has led us; delivering, upholding, defending, and restraining us when our wandering feet had almost slipped; when we see how near the edge of the precipice we had sometimes wandered, and were kept back by His hand, we shall exclaim, with adoring hearts, "He has done all things well."

The 23rd Psalm is the wilderness song of one who is proving the Lord as his Shepherd on the journey home. There the pilgrim is seen, with the cross (Psa 22) *behind* him, the glory (Psa 24) *before* him, and the Shepherd (Psa 23) *with* him. Although he is going through the "valley of the shadow of death" with enemies all around, yet he fears no evil, for the

Shepherd is by his side, and *His* rod, *His* staff, *His* guiding eye, are all available, until the pilgrim reaches "the house of the Lord", his everlasting home.

In the New Testament, there are also "wilderness" books. In the epistles to the Philippians and the Hebrews, and in the first Epistle of Peter, present day believers are addressed as in the wilderness with heaven before them,

Do you find this world a dreary wilderness? Do you not feel you are walking through a foreign land, where nothing can satisfy your heart, or attract your eye? Satan and your own heart will always seek to tempt and allure you into some side path, and bring to your remembrance the pleasures you have left behind in Egypt. Look up! The Man at the right hand of God is for you, and He can bring you through. Soon you shall reach the Father's house, and receive a hearty welcome there.

> *"There no stranger God shall meet thee,*
> *Stranger thou in courts above;*
> *He who to His rest shall greet thee,*
> *Greets thee with a well-known love."*

3. Israel in Canaan

They are now in the land flowing with milk and honey. The river Jordan has been crossed, the wilderness is past, and Egypt is far behind. They stand with swords in their hands now, a nation of warriors, taking possession of the land of which God had said, "Every place that the sole of your foot shall tread upon, that have I given you" (Josh 1:3). Theirs is no idle life: it is the "fight of faith". *Onward* is their watchword: led on by the Captain of the Lord's host (Josh 5.14), they will go from victory to victory.

This shows the believer as already risen, and seated in the heavenlies in Christ Jesus; not so much looking forward to heaven at the end of the journey, but spiritually there already; and already blessed with "all spiritual blessings in heavenly places in Christ" (Eph 1:3). The Epistle to the Ephesians may be called "The Believer's Canaan". There the expression *"heavenly places"* occurs often, and the believer is viewed as already there in Christ. Heaven, not earth, is the place of our inheritance and blessing. We are partakers of a *heavenly* calling (Heb 3:1), our citizenship is *heavenly* (Phil 3:20), and where our treasure is, there our heart is also.

Canaan is not really a type of what a believer enters after death when he departs to be with Christ, for there we shall be at rest. In Canaan we must handle the sword and shield, as in Ephesians 6, in conflict with wicked spirits who would dispute our right and hinder our enjoyment of what grace has given to us. We stand clad in the armour of God, like a soldier in the day of battle. If we abide "strong in the Lord and in the power of His might" we shall overcome. The "old corn of the land", type of Christ risen from the dead, is our daily food to strengthen us for the battle. This warfare is no child's play, but a downright contest with the devil. Christians who know most of their place and portion in Christ, will find this battle the hottest.

It is interesting to note that we are at the same time in Egypt, in the wilderness, and in Canaan. As a matter of *fact* we are in the world, and it is night. But "the night is far spent" (Rom 13:12), and we shall leave it finally in the morning, at the coming of the Lord. As to *experience,* we are in the wilderness; children still at school, under the Father's discipline and training. This is a lifelong lesson, only being perfected at the Lord's coming for us, or our going to be with Him. As to our *position* we are in Canaan, for while the world is around us and the flesh within us, in Christ we are far above both, and our standing is in Him. This is where we encounter the devil, and our conflict with him will cease only when, at the coming of the Lord, he is cast out of the heavens (Rev 12:9). But even now we are more than conquerors through Him who loved us (Rom 8:37). He won the fight for

17

us, and through us He triumphs still. Satan shall be bruised beneath our feet (Rom 16:20) - He cheers us on in the conflict by telling us this shall happen "shortly".

CHAPTER 3

Israel in Egypt - Sin's Slavery

The first chapter of the book of Exodus gives us a view of Israel in Egypt. There they are *slaves* of Pharaoh the Egyptian king, and also *idolaters* bowing down before Egypt's gods (Ezek 20:7-8). Their slavery was bitter and hard, making bricks for their merciless master, as the chapter shows. The taskmaster's whip and the clanking chain reveal their state, and show that they are under a power stronger than their own. They groan for deliverance, but they cannot escape. The strong man armed keeps his goods in peace (Luke 11:21).

Yet they had their little pleasures, for they speak of "the fish we did eat in Egypt freely, the cucumbers, the melons, the leeks, the onions, and the garlick" (Num 11:5). It would not have suited Pharaoh's purpose to have withheld these things from them, for they helped to keep them content with their lot, and to make them do his work more willingly.

This is a picture of the state of every unconverted sinner. Egypt is the type of this world (Rev 11:8); and Pharaoh is the type of Satan, who is its Prince and ruler (John 12:31; Eph 6:12). Man, by nature, is the slave of Satan; this present evil world is the scene of his slavery; and his sins are the chains that bind him. Man is sold under sin (Rom 7:14); he cannot deliver himself, for he is "without strength" (Rom 5:6). He is the tool of Satan, led *captive* by him at his will (2 Tim 2:26). It is, however, a willing bondage, for Satan has blinded his mind (2 Cor 4:4), and his understanding has been darkened (Eph 4:18), so that he thinks his bondage is liberty.

He cherishes the very sins that are his fetters now, and shall be the gnawing worm to agonise him in hell for ever. Oh, the cunning devices of the devil! He will even loosen the burden a little, and slacken the chains, to let his captive enjoy "the pleasures of sin for a season", in order that he may more securely bind and blind him for ever.

Satan is a skilled chain maker. His long experience has given him ample opportunity to watch the tastes of his victims, and provide a chain suited to each. Some are held by the iron chain of lust and passion, and go headlong to their doom; others with the more respectable chains of worldliness, the love of money, and the praise of men. Thus they are led silently but surely down to the pit. The drunkard's cup, the miser's money bag, and the hypocrite's cloak of false religion, alike suit Satan's purpose. A form of godliness, without conversion to God, may be the most potent tool of the devil, to delude and destroy a soul for eternity.

Here let me pause and ask if *you* have been delivered from Satan's yoke, or are you still his slave? Are you certain that no secret sin, loved and cherished, is noiselessly binding you to Satan and this world? Your conscience may be at ease and your peace undisturbed. The chain may have rusted upon you, but if you have not been set free by the Son of God, you are yet held fast in Satan's power, and he is leading you on to the lake of fire.

The captives toiling at Egypt's brick kilns had been seen by an eye in heaven; an ear had heard their groans; a heart had known their sorrows. The God of Abraham remembered His covenant and said, "I am come down to deliver them" (Exod 3:8). Blessed gospel tidings! If any help is given, it must "come down", for "no man can by any means redeem his brother" (Psa 49:7). "God so loved the world, that He gave His only begotten Son" (John 3:16), and, "Christ Jesus *came* into the world to save sinners" (1 Tim 1:15).

Here we have the answer to the type. God has been manifest in flesh, He has come down to deliver. By Christ's death on the Cross, He has bruised and conquered Satan. Death has been vanquished, and its sting taken away. The grave of Christ is empty, and He is seated on the right hand of God, with all power in heaven and on earth. He sends the gospel to the sinner's ear, proclaiming "liberty to the captive" and commands him to believe it. This gospel becomes "the power of God unto salvation, to every one that believeth" (Rom 1:16).

Do *you* believe the gospel? Have you opened your ear and heart, to receive the glad tidings? If you have, you are the Lord's freeman, and if the Son of God has made you *free,* you shall be "free indeed" (John 8:36).

CHAPTER 4

Pharaoh's Efforts - the Wiles of the Devil

Moses and Aaron have been commissioned from God and sent to Egypt. They go to its headquarters at once, and standing in the court of Pharaoh, amid the greatness and grandeur of Egypt, they present the demand of Jehovah, "Let My people go, that they may hold a feast to Me in the wilderness" (Exod 5:1).

But Pharaoh declares his open defiance at once. He orders the Israelites' burdens and tasks to be increased. He shows his contempt and hatred of God as he says, "Who is the Lord that I should obey His voice? I know not the Lord, neither will I let Israel go" (Exod 5:2).

This is Satan's way; it is the first of his plans to hinder the deliverance of a poor sinner. There is no disguise. It is the roar of the lion of hell, and open hostility to God and His truth. So long as the devil can keep his slaves at peace, quietly serving him, he does it. But when God begins to deal with the sinner to bring about his deliverance, immediately hell is let loose to hold on to him. Satan never gives up his prey without a struggle. At this point the sinner's state is worse than before (see Exod 5:15-23), for his conscience is awake, and he feels his chains. Eternity is revealed, and like the prodigal he has "come to himself" (Luke 15:17).

Let us now consider four ways or "wiles" of the devil (Eph 6:11) used to hinder or prevent the work of God.

The First Wile of the Enemy
The demand of Jehovah is pressed upon Pharaoh.

Judgements are falling on him and his land for refusal, so his tactics change. He sees that in open fight he cannot succeed, for "God is stronger than His foes". So he will try to accomplish his purpose by secret craftiness if he can. He calls Moses, and makes the concession, "Go ye, sacrifice to your God *in the land"* (Exod 8:25). This looks very gracious, it is a considerable stretch on Pharaoh's part. But it thinly veils the treachery of the devil. The aim of this piece of strategy is to destroy the very objective of the people's redemption, and their testimony to the true God. But Moses detected the plot, and immediately resisted it with the plain word of Jehovah, "We will go *three days' journey* into the wilderness, and sacrifice to our God *as He shall command us"* (Exod 8:27).

The word of God was definite. It could not, therefore, be compromised. The distance out of Egypt, where the altar of Jehovah was to stand, was measured by Jehovah Himself, and Moses could not lower the standard. He presents Jehovah's claims in full, in the face of the enemy.

Here then is one of the wiles of the devil. If, as a roaring lion, he cannot hinder the deliverance of a sinner by open opposition, as a subtle serpent he will endeavour to keep him sacrificing in Egypt. And has he not succeeded? Satan has no objection to anyone adopting a religion that keeps him as a decent worldling, "sacrificing in the land". Oh no, he will even give his patronage and applause to this. The world will speak well of such a person; he will be lauded and admired by all. Worldly religion embraces everything, and condemns nothing but wholeheartedness for Christ. It is conducted *"in the land"* on the principles of the world's charity; and being of the world, the world loves its own. But when the call of God is insisted on to march "three days' journey" into the wilderness - that is, the full length of the cross of Christ and what followed on "the third day", His resurrection, Satan will move all hell to hinder that. He hates an out-and-out separation to God. Full well he knows, that the one who acknowledges that he is dead and risen with Christ, bids farewell to him, his empire, his service, and his land for ever.

Professing Christian, have you taken "the three days' journey out of Egypt"? Are you separate from the world? Remember, you cannot bear a true testimony for God, or worship Him in truth, and at the same time have fellowship with worldlings, either in their sinful pleasures, or in their religion. "Ye cannot serve God and Mammon." The call of God is clear, "Come out from among them and be ye separate, saith the Lord" (2 Cor 6:17).

The Second Wile of the Enemy

"I will let you go, that ye may sacrifice to your God in the wilderness, *only ye shall not go very far away*" (Exod 8:28). This is hard pleading. It simply means, "Do not go out of my reach, but keep near enough to Egypt, so that I may without much trouble draw you back again, and thus destroy your testimony as a separated people." Borderland christianity is a grand tool for Satan; it suits his purpose well. A man that is neither out-and-out for God, nor yet a thorough worldling, is a stumbling-block to everybody. The world smiles with contempt at the man who prays in the prayer meeting one night, and sings at the concert the next. Honest people can easily gauge the depth of such a profession. They put him down as a hypocrite. He has no power at all for anything, but to make trouble. He is respected by no one, neither Christian nor worldling. His own conscience is defiled, his soul is vexed, and his whole appearance miserable. Lot was one of those who don't "go very far away". He tried to blend politics and piety while living in Sodom, and the people mocked him. His worldliness entirely paralysed his preaching. His children married people from Sodom, and in the end he was dragged out of Sodom, saved as by fire, to end his days in a lonely cave with a blighted life and testimony.

24

Young believer, Satan will try this stratagem with you. He will whisper, "Don't go too far. There's no need to be tightlaced. You may be a Christian and sing an innocent worldly song, take a dance, or enjoy a bit of pleasure. There are many good christian people who see no harm in doing these things. We must not make ourselves peculiar. We must be like other people." All this style of reasoning is from the devil. By it he wishes to blunt the testimony of saints for God in the world, and drag them down to the level of carnal religious men. We are distinctly told, however, in God's Book, that His people are a *"peculiar people"* (1 Pet 2:9), that they are not to walk "as other Gentiles" (Eph 4:17; 1 Cor 3:3). So dear saints of God, resist the devil, steadfast in the faith! Contend for "the three days' journey" in all your ways. Let the cross and grave of Christ be the measure of your separation from the world. This is God's christianity.

The Third Wile of the Enemy

"Go ye now that are men" (Exod 10:11). Poor Pharaoh is in sore trouble. The hand of God is coming heavier and heavier upon him. He stretches a bit further. He will now let them go the "three days' journey", but wants the "little ones" left behind. This is clever work. Parents in the wilderness worshipping Jehovah, and children left in Egypt, beside its idolaters! What a spectacle, too! What a testimony! Well did Pharaoh know that if he succeeded in this, his end would be gained. He knew that if the "little ones" were left, the parents would soon return. Alas many christian parents have forgotten this, and left their children in the world, engrossed in its pleasures, and running in its course unrestrained. The testimony of many christian parents has been spoiled, by leaving their little ones in Egypt, encouraging them to be involved in its activities and learn its ways, in the company of the most ungodly people. Lot and Eli were both of this class, and the judgement of God that fell on their families, stands as a warning to all who follow that road.

The Last Wile of the Enemy

Pharaoh is hard pressed, and he makes a last attempt. It is very feeble, nevertheless if he can hold on to anything and only keep one slender link unbroken, he may gain by it. "Go ye, serve the Lord, only let your flocks and herds be stayed, let your little ones also go with you" (Exod 10:24). Pharaoh is now very accommodating. He will be easily pleased. His demands seem reasonable. Flocks and herds would be burdensome on a journey. Would it not be better to leave them? Moses says No! Although personally the meekest man on earth, he was one of the Lord's "invincibles". He would not yield one iota of God's demands. Flocks and herds must be Jehovah's too. He must have all. And so Pharaoh got the final and decisive answer, "There shall not a hoof be left behind" (Exod 10:26).

This was the divine demand. It could not be conceded. Not a point could be yielded. Jehovah must have His own. Decision gained the victory, and the enemy, foiled at every point, was obliged to retreat defeated.

Young believer, let your watchword be *decision for Christ*. Never attempt to lower the claims of God upon you. Yield nothing to Satan as you carry them out. Never mind what others do, you render obedience to every word of God. Resist the devil and he will flee from you. Be like Moses who would not lower the claims of Jehovah; like Daniel who would rather enter the lion's den than disobey his God; like the three Hebrew young men, who went into the fiery furnace rather than worship an image set up by earth's greatest monarch. They lost nothing by their faithfulness, for God has said, "Them that honour Me, I will honour" (1 Sam 2:30). Entire separation to God is the divine standard: no half-heartedness, no half-way house. Worship, little ones, business and all, must go the three days' journey, and bear the mark of resurrection life, which is *separation to God.*

CHAPTER 5

Death of the Firstborn

God's final judgement upon Egypt was pronounced in a few solemn words. "I will pass through the land of Egypt this night, and will smite *all* the firstborn in the land of Egypt, both man and beast, and against all the gods of Egypt I will execute judgment: I am the Lord" (Exod 12:12).

In the other plagues Israel had been exempt, but in this one there is no difference between Israel and Egypt. All have sinned, all must die. "The wages of sin is death." God, as a holy Judge, must execute judgement without respect of persons on all who deserve it. In the silent midnight hour, the time when they would least expect it, the awful judgement would come.

The judgement of this world will be like this. In longsuffering grace and love, God postpones it meanwhile, for He has no delight in the condemnation of the sinner. But its hour must come. Wrath long held back, will burst in awful fury on the Christless and the God-forgetting crowd. The day is appointed and the sentence is recorded. It will be executed when men are least expecting it. As a thief in the night, suddenly, swiftly, like the lightning's flash, the Lord Jesus shall be revealed from heaven in flaming fire, "taking vengeance on them that know not God and obey not the Gospel" (2 Thess 1:7-8). Things will go on as in the days before the judgement of the flood in Noah's time. The world will continue on its course, buying, selling, and sinning, till all shall be brought to a dead halt, by the appearance of the rejected Jesus of Nazareth in the clouds of heaven.

"There was a great cry in Egypt" (Exod 12:30). It was the cry of agony and despair from a people now feeling the weight of Jehovah's rod. It is the echo of a deeper wail, a more terrible cry, that shall one day be wrung from the lips of the Christ-despising crowd, when they plead for rocks and hills to hide them from the face of Him that sits on the throne, and from the wrath of the Lamb (Rev 6:16). But that pleading will go unheeded. The unresponsive rocks will mock their prayer, and He that sitteth in the heavens shall "laugh at his calamity, and mock when his fear cometh" (Prov 1:26). Their call for mercy has come too late. What a terrible prospect this is for the sinner who has rejected Christ as saviour.

For Israel's first-born sons, however, a ransom was provided. A salvation and a deliverance was wrought, as we shall consider in our next chapter.

CHAPTER 6

The Passover

Exodus 12 has been aptly named "The Picture Book of Redemption". It is one of the fullest, clearest, and simplest foreshadowings in the Old Testament of salvation by the blood of the Lamb. This is the grand theme of all of Holy Scripture, from Abel's lamb offered on the altar outside Eden, to the cross of the Lamb of God, outside the walls of Jerusalem. The prophets spoke much about it, the tabernacle and temple ceremonies pointed to it, and psalmists sang about it; and the melody of heaven's new song shall ever be "Thou hast redeemed us to God by *Thy blood*".

A bloodless religion is a sinner's ruin. It was first instituted by Cain the murderer, and perpetuated by all his seed. Many preachers and professors of the present century still curl the lip and sneer at what they call a "religion of the shambles". But they need to be reminded that "without shedding of blood there is no remission" (Heb 4:22), and that a religion without blood is a sure title to hell and the lake of fire.

We will now look at this precious type set out in the passover. Every aspect is perfect, every part full of the deepest meaning. We know that it speaks of Jesus, for it is written "Christ *our passover is sacrificed* for us" (1 Cor 5:7).

1. The Lamb
It was to be without blemish, and "a male of the first year". These are emblems of meekness, purity, and strength. Such was Jesus. He "was led as a lamb to the slaughter", and for the hands that shed His blood He sought forgiveness. He

29

was "without blemish". Had there been a spot found in Him, He would have been unfit for sacrifice. But Jesus was perfect. He "*did* no sin" (1 Pet 2:22). He "*knew* no sin" (2 Cor 5:21*)*. "*In* Him was no sin" (1 John 3:5).

He was perfect as the baby of Bethlehem, perfect as the boy of Nazareth, perfect as the Son of Man, and perfect as the Lamb of God on the Cross. He died in the full vigour of His manhood. He was the Son of God from the bosom of the Father, "mighty to save".

"Ye shall keep it up until the fourteenth day" (Exod 12:6). This was the testing time. It gave ample opportunity to find out any blemish, if any had been there. So Jesus was well tried. His life on earth was the testing time. Heaven, earth, and hell tried Him, and we have the witness from each that He is the Lamb "without blemish". The *Father* testified from heaven: "This is My beloved Son in whom I am well pleased" (Matt 3:17). The *demons* cried, "I know Thee who Thou art, the Holy One of God" (Mark 1:24); and He came forth unscathed from the temptation in the wilderness when the devil's wiles were used against Him, in the most unfavourable circumstances (Matt 4:11). *Man* testified also. Pilate, the Roman governor, said, "I find in Him no fault at all" (John 18:38). Judas, the false disciple, confessed that he had betrayed the innocent blood (Matt 27:4). The centurion who watched His dying agonies, owned that He was a "righteous man" (Luke 23:47). The dying robber by His side, confessed that He had done "nothing amiss" (Luke 23:41). Thus His very enemies bore witness that Jesus, the Lamb was "without blemish". Precious, perfect, spotless Lamb of God, without blemish and without spot!

2. The Manner and Time of its Death

"The whole assembly of the congregation of Israel shall kill it, in the evening" (Exod 12:6).

Every sinner had a hand in the death of Jesus. The world was represented around His cross: "Against Thy holy child

Jesus, whom Thou hast anointed, both Herod and Pontius Pilate, with the Gentiles and the people of Israel, were gathered together" (Acts 4:27). The representatives of man's wisdom, man's power, and man's religion were all there, each alike against Him, as witnessed by the inscription in Hebrew, Greek, and Latin upon His Cross. They differed in many things, but in this they were all agreed that the Son of God ought to die. Herod and Pilate who before were enemies, shook hands over His death (Luke 23:12).

The Lamb was slain in the *evening,* the judgement came at *midnight.* There was just time to sprinkle the blood, but no time to delay. This is the day of the reign of grace, but the *midnight,* dark with judgement, is approaching rapidly.

3. The Use Made of the Blood

The blood was put into a basin, and a bunch of hyssop was prepared to apply it. See now the picture of a sinner's salvation. "And ye shall take of the blood and strike it on the two side posts, and on the upper door posts of the houses...and the blood shall be to you for a token upon the houses where ye are, and when I see the blood I will pass over you" (Exod 12:7-13).

It was the blood on the lintel and doorposts - and *the blood* alone - that secured the salvation of Israel's firstborn sons on that awful night. It was not the living lamb, tied to the door post, nor even the blood in the basin, but the blood applied and sprinkled on the door where the first-born lived - the blood appropriated and applied by the bunch of hyssop. It was not the blood and the bitter herbs, nor the blood and the unleavened bread, but the blood of the lamb *alone,* that saved the first-born sons from judgement.

Nor was it their happy feelings, nor their pilgrim clothing, that made them sure of salvation. Their *assurance* rested on something infinitely better than any of these temporary and shifting things. They were assured of salvation by the word of the eternal God, for *He* had said, "When I see the blood I will pass over you." This was enough. They were safe from the destroying angel's sword, as safe as if they had been standing in the land of Canaan.

How is it with *your* soul? Have you taken refuge underneath the precious blood of Christ? Do you believe it was shed for you, and that God has accepted the sacrifice. He sees the blood, He knows its true value and worth, and He says to all who have put their trust in it and in Him, "I will pass over you." Does He speak the truth? If he does, you are safe. Never mind doubts and fears and changing feelings which you may have.

What did it matter to a blood-sheltered Israelite, how he *felt,* or what he *feared,* so long as God was true to His word, "*I will pass over you.*" Neither fears nor feelings could ever make that word untrue. The blood of Christ alone is the ground of *salvation,* and the written Word of God is the ground of *assurance.* The blood is Godward, the word is manward. None of the blood was put upon the threshold, or sprinkled on the floor. No, it was too costly to be trampled under foot. Yet sinners are treading under foot the Son of God, and counting His blood worthless (Heb 10:29). They are making a stepping-stone to hell of the fact that Jesus died. The corrupt christianity of the present acknowledges the fact that Christ died. Many believe that fact, but it is like the blood of the paschal Lamb in the basin: it is not used, it is not appropriated by faith. They are not saved because they have not sprinkled it, they have not believed in its power and applied it to their souls' need.

How do you treat the blood of Christ? Are you safe, or exposed? Is it above your head, accepted; or beneath your feet, rejected ?

CHAPTER 7

The Feast of the Redeemed

When the prodigal son returned to his father's heart and home, he was sat down at a well spread table to share a feast of joy (Luke 15:21-24). The kiss, the robe, the ring, and the shoes were not all that was provided. Once at rest in his father's love, his doubts and fears removed, the son heard his glad father say, "Let us eat and be merry." So the blesser and the blessed, the rejoicing father and the welcomed son, sat down together to feast upon the fatted calf.

When the Jewish ruler's daughter was raised to life by the Lord Jesus, He commanded that something should be given her to eat (Luke 8:55). When sinners are brought into newness of life and welcomed to the heart and household of God, their bliss is crowned by being made partakers of the children's bread. They are called to the fellowship of the Father and His Son Jesus Christ, a fellowship known and enjoyed even here below, and which will be yet more fully known in the presence of God above, where sin can never mar it, nor anything hinder its flow.

The feast prepared for Israel while sheltering under the bloodstained lintel in Egypt is the type of this. Their deliverance from judgement had been secured by the sprinkled blood on the lintel and side posts outside. Inside the homes of these ransomed people all was peace and joy, in spite of the scenes of awful despair all around them outside. The redeemed were gathered around a table, each one ready for a journey, a staff in everyone's hand. They were fully occupied feeding on the lamb during the hours of that eventful night. It was not spent in cool indifference, nor unconscious slumber.

There is an important lesson for us. We have been left in this dark world for a little while, to hold communion with the Son of God. This is the highest privilege of all the Lord's redeemed people.

Young believer, you have known the meaning of the blood-stained lintel. Now what do you know of the spread table? Is it your daily habit to live in communion with God? Do you spend your time feeding on Christ? God has given the blood of Christ to answer the claims of your awakened conscience, and now it is at rest, perfect rest. He has also given you the person of Christ to satisfy your longing heart. Your heart will be truly happy when it delights itself in the Lord, needing no other cheer and no other joy.

The eating of the Lamb
"They shall eat the flesh in that night, roast with fire, and unleavened bread; and with bitter herbs they shall eat it. Eat not of it raw, nor sodden at all with water, but roast with fire; his head with his legs, and the purtenance thereof" (Exod 12:8-9).

Jesus is the Lamb of God. Roasting with fire reminds us of the suffering He endured from the hand of God. We feed upon a suffering Christ. We have fellowship with Jesus as the suffering one. And what a feast this is! How tender it makes the conscience! How it moves and fills the heart with deepest love to Him! As we think of His dying agony, the anguish of His soul upon the tree, His deep and mighty love that many waters could not quench nor floods drown, we love Him in return. Our heart is won, our affections are engaged, and Jesus, Jesus only, becomes the object of our admiration and worship, the theme of our sweetest song. All else grows dim, the world loses its attraction; the soul recoils from its pleasures because it has found a far better portion, and it is satisfied, abundantly satisfied.

The Lamb was eaten with *bitter herbs*. Eaten by themselves these are so unsavoury, but not when eaten with the roast lamb. The "bitter herbs" have been spoken of as representing sorrow for sin. And surely at no time does sin appear so exceedingly sinful, as when we are in communion with the Lord. There the mask is dropped, and sin is seen in its true character in the light of the cross. We remember whose sins they were that brought the blessed Saviour there, and beneath whose load He died. Our heart melts and our tears flow, tears of true love too - a tribute of affection to the One who died. Grace alone can work true repentance; love alone can win the rebel sinner's heart; and where that grace and love are truly known, such sorrow for sin, and hatred of it too, will not be found wanting.

Many seeking souls have put the "bitter herbs" in the place of the sprinkled blood. They have sought to find peace with God by being sorry for the past, instead of trusting in the blood of Christ alone. In this condition they have gone on for years, hoping their hard hearts would melt, and that they would feel love to God rising within them. But such love is foreign to the heart of fallen man, nor can he ever put it there. It is only by accepting God's love for us, revealed in Christ, that we can really feel and express love to Him.

> *"Then a sense of blood-bought pardon*
> *Soon dissolves a heart of stone."*

Unleavened bread completed the feast. Its meaning we find in 1 Corinthians 5:8, "The unleavened bread of sincerity and truth". Leaven was not to be eaten, nor to be allowed in the house. In the Bible it is a type of evil, always evil, only evil; and of such evil as slowly and gradually works in upon the believer, defiling and destroying the vitals of his christian life. We read of the "leaven of malice and wickedness" (1 Cor 5:8); "the leaven of the Pharisees"- hypocrisy (Luke 12:1); "the leaven of the Sadducees"- rationalism (Matt 16:6-12); and "the leaven of Herod"- politics (Mark 8:15). If a believer allows or practises these evils, he will not be able to enjoy communion with Christ. In days like these, when such leavening influences are at their deadly work among men, the saints need to watch lest they also become defiled.

The *attitude* of the feasting person is also significant: "Thus shall ye eat it; with your *loins* girded, your *shoes* on your feet, and your *staff* in your hand; and ye shall eat it in haste; it is the Lord's passover" (Exod 12:11). This was evidently a pilgrims' attitude. They were eating the feast, but on the tiptoe of expectation, waiting for the signal to depart. They stood as strangers in a strange land, but their home was waiting for them on the other side.

We are pilgrims and strangers on earth; at least so we sing. But do we live as if we believed it? Are we always ready and listening to hear that voice that shall call us away? But, ready or not, the hour will come when "the Lord Himself shall descend with a shout", and the living saints, together with the dead in Christ, shall be caught up to meet Him. Earth, so poor, shall be left behind, and we shall go to be at home with the Lord.

Thus saved by the blood, assured of salvation by the Word, communing with the Father and the Son by the Spirit, let us stand like girded men who wait for their Lord, saying, "Even so come, Lord Jesus."

CHAPTER 8

The Memorial Feast

The feast instituted on the night of Israel's deliverance was to be observed by them throughout all their generations. They were ever to have in remembrance their redemption by the blood of the paschal lamb. Even after the wilderness was past, and they had settled in the land flowing with milk and honey, the memorial feast was to be kept. Doubtless it pointed onward (as do all the types) to Calvary, but it was also for them the memorial of a redemption and deliverance already past.

What the feast of the Passover was to Israel, the Lord's Supper in many respects is to the Christian now. Of course there are many points in contrast, as grace is to law, and Christianity to Judaism. The Passover was the memorial of the deliverance of an earthly people, the Lord's Supper commemorates the redemption and call of a heavenly people. The Passover was eaten by a nation circumcised in the flesh, the Lord's Supper is for those who reckon themselves dead to the flesh, and now live to God in the Spirit.

There are three points connected with the Passover as found in the Scriptures which we shall consider one at a time: 1. its institution by Jehovah at the first, and the obedience of His people in observing it; 2. its corruption, or the devil's imitation of God's Passover and how the people of God were drawn into the snare; 3. the restoration of Jehovah's original feast at various stages, according to the measure of His peoples' light and faithfulness.

1. It was "the Lord's Passover" (Exod 12:11).

It was a "Feast of Jehovah" (Lev 23:4). Therefore His Word alone must guide, His commands alone must be obeyed. They were to be observed unaltered by Israel's seed "for ever". Similarly the New Testament feast is *"The Lord's Supper"*. It is not the believer's "own Supper", nor the "Church's Supper", or else their voices might be listened to, and their opinions taken into account. But it is the Supper of Him who is now "Lord and Christ", so the loyal heart will bow to His will, and recognise no other authority. Who gave man a right to meddle with what is the Lord's? Can He not order His own table and rule His own house, apart from the interference of the "will of man"? We firmly believe He can.

In the days of the Lord's life on earth, the feast of the Passover had deteriorated to a mere religious form. The traditions of men had so set aside the commandments of the Lord, that it had entirely lost its character. Speaking of it, Jesus called it "the Jews' Passover", "a feast of the Jews" (John 2:13; 5:1).   It was no longer a "Feast of Jehovah", no more "the Lord's Passover". Jehovah will not identify His name with a sham, or give it His approval. There is a lesson to learn here. People may gather round a table to break bread and drink wine; they may keep a feast and call it by the Lord's name, and yet because of man's traditions and human rule and presidency at the table, this may not be "the Lord's Supper". The Lord's Supper can only be rightly observed where Christ's Lordship and His Word are the only recognised authorities.

It was for all the Lord's people (Exod 12:47), unless perchance, some were defiled, as in Numbers 9:6. If an Israelite neglected to keep the feast, he was "cut off from among his people" (Num 9:13).   To neglect the keeping of the feast incurred the Lord's displeasure, just as keeping it "unclean" or "with leaven" would have done. This needs to be noted in our day, when the Lord's Supper is often neglected and believers absent themselves from it because of some paltry excuse. Surely if in a day of "shadows" and a "worldly sanctuary" reverence and subjection were required of the Lord's redeemed people in the keeping of His feast, much more ought it to be now, where the saints are gathered in the light of the Divine presence, and where "Jesus in the midst" is *Lord*.

A believer who is defiled either by contact with evil all around, or by allowing the flesh to defile him from within, ought not to go to the Lord's Supper in this condition. Some at Corinth evidently did so, and the Lord judged them by weakness, sickness, and death (1 Cor 11:29,30). But for defiled ones a gracious provision has been made. For the Israelites defiled by the dead, there was the "water of separation" (see Numbers 9 and 19), and for believers now, self-judgement and confession before the Lord will restore fellowship with Him (see 1 John 1:8,9).

It was not for the foreigner and the hired servant (Exod 12:45). The Lord's Supper is not for the unconverted, whose condition is that of "strangers and foreigners" (Eph 2:19). No unconverted communicant was at the Feast when it was instituted by the Lord. Judas Iscariot went out before it began (compare Matthew 26 with John 13), and we also read that the disciples "continued in the breaking of bread" (Acts 2:42), and "of the rest (i.e. the unconverted) durst no man join himself to them"(5:13*)*.

But nowadays very often the unconverted "parishioner" claims his seat at "the sacrament" as he does his place in other things. In most of the churches and chapels in christendom unconverted folk go to "the sacrament" expecting to get salvation, or in some way to be made ready for heaven by this "means of grace". Poor souls, working hard to earn the salvation that God says is a gift, this "sacrament taking" helps them on in their sad delusion. Some of God's people are mixed up with this, and by giving it their patronage and support, they help on the ruin of souls.

It was to be kept at the Lord's appointed place. When Israel reached the land, the Lord chose a place to put His Name there. The worshipper was to bring his offering there (Deut 12:14), and *there* he was to keep the Passover. (See Deut 16:5-6.) The city chosen was Jerusalem. There the feast was to be kept, for there the Lord had put His Name (see 2 Chron 6:5-6), and thither the tribes went up to "the testimony of Israel" (Psa 122:4). On the fourteenth day of the first month, year by year, the people of Israel might have been seen leaving their homes and gathering together to the "City of the Great King" to keep the memorial feast. It was a beautiful sight telling of true-heartedness to Jehovah and obedience to His Word. Thus too the early disciples, in obedience to their absent Lord's request, "This do in remembrance of Me," persisted in gathering together to *His Name,* there to eat the Lord's Supper. There was one gathering point - "the Name of the Lord Jesus Christ"; and one feast - the Lord's Supper. All the saints were together (Acts 2:44). There were no sects or rival churches, in those days.

> *"The saints were of one heart and soul,*
> *And love to Christ inspired the whole."*

The time to keep the feast: Once a year - the fourteenth day of the first month - was God's appointed time to keep the feast. To have kept it twice in the year, or once in two, would have been disobedience. To do what God commands is obedience, and nothing else is. The word in connection with the Supper is, "This do ye, as *oft* as ye drink it in remembrance of Me; for as *often* as ye eat this bread and drink this cup ye do show the Lord's death *till He come"* (1 Cor 11:25,26). The church, in her early love, kept the feast on the first day of every week (see Acts 20:7), and this is our example. Anyone who thinks that once a quarter, or once a year, is often enough to show forth His death must have a cold heart for the Lord Jesus. "As seldom" as ye do it, would be a more fitting word for such conduct, and yet this is the practice of thousands who claim to be Christians.

So we have seen that the order of the feast - the guests, the place, and the time, have all been arranged by the Lord; and loving hearts delight to know that His will is still the same, and are joyfully ready to do it.

2. The Devil's Counterfeit: God's People were Ensnared.

Wherever God does a work on earth, Satan first tries to oppose it, and next to corrupt it by introducing a sham. This is what Jeroboam, a king of the ten tribes of Israel, did in later years. He was an idol worshipper. It would not have suited his purpose, however, to introduce idolatry in a barebones fashion! He ingeniously contrived another plan to draw away the people from God's king and city. He decided to set up a complete set of counterfeits of all God's institutions for His people's worship: altars at Dan and Bethel, in connection with calves of gold, manmade priests from among the lowest of the people, and a passover *like* unto the feast at Jerusalem, on the fifteenth day of the eight month. It was a complete set of diabolical shams, "devised", we are told, *"out of his own heart"* (1 Kings 12:33). *Sham* altars, with *sham* priests officiating and a *sham* feast at a *wrong* time; and the people turned from God's reality, to Satan's counterfeit, as many always do, until "the feast of the Lord" gradually disappeared, and the devil's counterfeit became the order of the day.

In connection with the Lord's Supper a similar counterfeit can easily be discerned by those who will take their Bibles and compare what God has there commanded with what goes by the name of the Lord's Supper in christendom, sometimes called the "sacrifice of the mass" or the communion service or the sacrament. Where is the Scripture authority for the annual or half-yearly sacrament, accessible to all the members of the sect in which it is observed, whether converted or not? Where in the Book of God do we read of an officiating "minister" dispensing the sacrament and "administering the ordinance", or of appointed "Fast Days" to prepare the carnal and ungodly to "go forward" to this "means of grace"?

All God's people who are in association with these things must surely see that they are in direct antagonism to the revealed will of the Lord. But it is not enough to see it and even mourn over it. God has put within our reach the ability to do His will, and so every saint needs to wake up and act, rather than to sit and say, "We must take things as we find them." This may suit lukewarm, worldly people - but it is refreshing to see in the Scriptures men of a different spirit, such as Hezekiah, Josiah, and Nehemiah, who not only mourned over the ruin, but set themselves to work to effect a restoration.

3. Restoration of the Feast: the Work of Reformers

Hezekiah was the first of these reformers. His father was an idolater, and things in the kingdom were at their worst (see 2 Chron 28). Nevertheless, he was not daunted, but set to work at once. "He clave to the Lord, and departed not from His commandments" (2 Kings 18:6); and when a man is obedient to the light he has, God gives him more.

He began by demolishing idolatry, cleansing the house of the Lord, and setting men and things in their true places, according to the light he had. Next he dealt with the Passover. He sent letters to "all Israel and Judah, to come up to Jerusalem to *keep the Passover* unto the Lord God of Israel, for they had not done it of a long time in such sort as it was written" (2 Chron 30:1,5). This was a bold step, and could scarcely be expected to meet the universal approval of a backslidden people. So the thing was laughed to scorn, and the messengers were mocked (30:10). But some felt the rebuke, humbled themselves and came, and they kept the feast with great joy, as it had not been kept since the days of Solomon (30:26). This was true rejoicing, and a step in the right direction.

Josiah was the next. When little more than a boy, he began to search the longlost Book of the Law (2 Chronicles 34), and he found there that things were not at all as they ought to be. So he set to work. The Passover was kept on the fourteenth day of the first month, the right time; and in Jerusalem, the right place. Great joy and blessing followed, for there was no Passover like it from the days of Samuel the prophet (2 Chron 35:18).

This was a further advance; but the days of Samuel were not the "great original" of Exodus 12. A long pause followed. Judah was carried captive to Babylon - the temple was destroyed - the people sat in darkness and sorrow in Babylon, till Ezra and Nehemiah arrived on the scene. The mass of the nation saw Jerusalem no more; but a remnant arose and went back to Jerusalem with the Book of God in their hands. They commenced to set things in order "as it is written in the law of Moses, the man of God" (Ezra 3:2).

This was true ground to take. Back to the beginning - away past Solomon and Samuel, and a long list of other "good men" right back to what was "written in the law of Moses". This is the only firm rock on which to plant our feet. "Thus saith the Lord" is that on which we must take our stand. Good men are not our pattern, for although we may revere their memory, it is beyond all dispute that they have made great mistakes. For example, it was Aaron, the good High Priest of Israel, who set up the golden calf, and wicked Jeroboam could point to his example as authority for his calves at Dan and Bethel. You see where we may find ourselves if we follow men. God and His Word alone are infallible. We must act upon that Word, as they did in Ezra 6:19-22.

The Passover was kept according to Exodus 12. Although only a handful were there, yet it was kept with joy, "for the Lord had made them joyful". This was true recovery. Not anything new, but the old thing, the original thing revived, at least in miniature. No doubt it was but a small affair compared with the great days of the beginning, and we read that they wept as well as sang (Ezra 3:11,12). But they had a "little strength" and they spent it for God. This is what we are called to do in regard to the Lord's Supper. We are not to coin a new feast, or copy the Reformers or the great men of other days, but go back to the Word of God for the original. There has been much blessed truth recovered during the last three or four centuries, as Hezekiah and Josiah so far recovered the Passover; but the danger has been to settle down at every step gained, and establish a creed as so many have done. But the *whole* Word of God, apart from the traditions of men, must be our guide. We read in that Book that "on the first day of the week, the disciples came together to break bread" (Acts 20:7); that "they came together into one place to eat the Lord's Supper" (1 Cor 11:20); and that this is to be continued "till He come" (1 Cor 11:26). We may be only a feeble remnant of the scattered sheep of the blood-bought flock of God, yet in conscious weakness we gather to the Great Shepherd, owning Him as Lord at His own table, and joyfully respond to the request of His loving heart: *"This do in remembrance of Me."*

CHAPTER 9

Departure from Egypt

Closely connected with the people's salvation from the destroying angel's sword was their departure and separation from the land of Egypt. The same night on which the blood of the paschal lamb was sprinkled on their lintels and door-posts, they turned their backs on Egypt, its people, and its gods. They said farewell to the scenes of their idolatry and slavery for ever. Every link that had bound them was snapped, and they went free to serve the living and true God. How solemn and how dramatic their departure from that doomed country must have been! At the hour of midnight, while the Egyptians wailed over their dead first-born, they rose and silently hurried away, thousands of slaves now set free.

"Egypt was glad when they departed" (Psa 105:38), and Pharaoh urged them away from among his people. Truly they might say, "By strength of hand, the Lord brought us forth from Egypt, from the house of bondage" (Exod 13:14); and He who led them out, could never lead them back again.

The believer's separation from the world is closely linked with his salvation. We read of "Jesus Christ, who gave Himself for our sins, that He might deliver us from this present evil world, according to the will of God and our Father" (Gal 1:3-4). The cross of Christ is the door of escape from a doomed world, as well as the place of refuge for a guilty sinner. By the cross the believer is crucified to the world, and separated unto God.

Many people do not see this, or do not want to see it. They

speak of the cross as their deliverance from the wrath to come, but ignore its power to separate them from the world. They live at home in Egypt, associating with the ungodly; and although they speak of being in heaven at last, they grasp as much of the world as they can, or to use a popular phrase, they try "to make the best of both worlds". It is not "the will of God and our Father" that His children should be mixed up in alliance with the world. He has spoken on this with a clearness that none need mistake. What do you think of this verse: "Ye adulterers and adulteresses, know ye not that the friendship of the world is enmity with God? whosoever, therefore, will be a friend of the world is the enemy of God" (James 4:4)? This does not read like "making the best of both worlds" does it? Nor has anyone who ever tried to do so found the game to be a gaining one, either for time or for eternity.

We learn then from this part of Israel's history how the Lord separates His redeemed people from this present evil world. Make the line of separation a clear one. Let the gap between you and the world be as wide as God has made it. The *"mixed multitude"* (Exod 12:38) may teach us another lesson. If one trick fails, the enemy will try another, for his devices are not one, but many. If he cannot retain some of God's redeemed people in Egypt, he will send Egyptians up to Canaan mixed up among them. And has he not succeeded? In the dead of night, it would have been a difficult thing to detect a few Egyptians among a band of some two million people. Probably this mixture consisted of the Egyptian friends of Israelite families, for it would appear they had intermarried (see Lev 24:10), and what more natural than to accompany their friends? But these became a weakness and a curse to them. It was the "mixed multitude" who cried for flesh, and loathed the manna, and they led Israel to do the same (Num 11:4; 21:5).

And so it ever is. During a time of soul saving, Satan introduces his counterfeits, and sends them on along with the Lord's redeemed. They may go on well for a time, but by and by they come out in their true colours - always leaving their marks among the people of God. Some follow for the "loaves and the fishes", and others are led on by natural feelings; and none more likely than the relations and friends of true believers, who have outwardly adopted the profession and name of Christian through their influence. Such will only become a drag and a snare to the true believer; therefore let us watch the worldlings, who "unawares creep in" among the saints. Sooner or later, they will return to the world, and their influence for evil is great indeed.

"And they borrowed of the Egyptians jewels of silver, and jewels of gold, and raiment. And the Lord gave the people favour in the sight of the Egyptians, so that they lent unto them such things as they required, and they spoiled the Egyptians" (Exod 12:36). Some have been puzzled with these verses, and an evil use has been made of them by others, to show that it is right thing to "fleece" the world, and take its goods and money to be used in the work of the Lord, as these jewels evidently were in the building of the tabernacle, or perhaps for the making of the golden calf (Exodus 32). But these words will bear no such meaning. "Borrowed" and "lent" in this case mean "asked" and "given"; and when they did receive, it was only their hard-earned wages for years of unpaid work in brickmaking. These verses cannot justify begging sermons, religious raffles, bazaars, etc. to raise money to carry on a "cause" or to erect magnificent buildings where man's pride may figure and his vanity be exhibited under the guise of religion.

May God's people be kept from the spirit of such things, as well as from fellowship with them. To work for a worldly master and receive due wages, or to hire an ungodly servant and pay him for his work, is right; but to borrow from the world and not pay, or to go in debt with the world, or beg from it, is against the plain teaching of the Word of God (Rom 13:7-8; 2 Cor 8:21).

CHAPTER 10

The Pillar of Cloud and Fire

As sinners we need a *Saviour,* as captives we need a *Deliverer,* and as pilgrims we need a *Guide.* So the God of love, who from highest heaven saw our lost condition and gave His Son to be our Saviour and Deliverer, has also in His further grace and goodness given us His Holy Spirit and His Word to guide us. Father, Son, and Holy Spirit have all been engaged in the work of our salvation; and they are all also engaged in bringing us home to our rest above.

Israel was encamped in Etham, on the edge of the wilderness, not knowing a step of the road that lay between them and their home in Canaan. How it must have gladdened their hearts to see the pillar of cloud descend (Exod 13:20-22). Unasked, and we may say unexpected, God came down in the cloudy pillar to be their guide; to walk with them, to defend them, and to be their companion. What though the way be long and dreary, and the "great and terrible wilderness" is beset with dangers and filled with fiery serpents and scorpions, so long as God is with them! Every step and every danger are well known to Him, and if they only follow where He leads them, all will be well for them.

In the daytime the cloud was a covering, stretching over the entire camp, to screen them from the heat. As the shades of evening fell, it became a pillar of fire to give them light (Psa 105:39). So they were never in darkness. To travel by night was as easy as by day, for the Lord God gave them light, and "there was no night there". How faithfully and lovingly He performed His guiding work as the Shepherd of

Israel. The words of Deuteronomy 33:10-12 tell us: "He found him in a desert land, and in the waste howling wilderness; He *led* him about. He *instructed* him. He *kept* him as the apple of His eye. As an eagle stirreth up her nest, fluttereth over her young, spreadeth abroad her wings, taketh them, beareth them on her wings; so the Lord alone did lead him, and there was no strange god with him." Their failures, their murmurings, and their sins did not drive Him away, nor make Him withdraw the cloudy pillar from them. It accompanied them all the forty years of their pilgrimage and hovered above them as they marched in triumph through the dried-up bed of Jordan. At last it found its rest amidst the glories of the temple in the land. And "this God is *our* God for ever and ever". He will do all this for us and more besides!

The three positions of the cloud tell us of God *for* us, God *with* us, and God *in* us. At the Red Sea it stood between them and their enemies, the Egyptians - God was fighting for them (Exod 14:19); as they walked through the desert, it went before them to seek out a resting-place - He was always with them (Num 9:17); and in the tabernacle it rested in their midst - His presence was in the centre of them all (Exod 40:34). When the cloud moved they followed; when it rested so did they. Jehovah was their Leader and King. It was His to command; it was theirs to obey. He was the Shepherd, they were the sheep. And He who guided Israel across the dreary desert by the pillar of cloud and fire, has not left us unprovided for. He has given us *His Spirit* and *His Word.* These are to be our pillar of cloud and fire till our desert days are done and our journey is over. In their light we shall walk safely and securely - we shall walk with God and walk worthy of the Lord (Col 1:10).

Of the Word, it is written, "Thy Word is a *lamp* unto my feet, and a *light* unto my path" (Psa 119:105); and of the Spirit, "He shall *guide* you into all truth, and *show* you things to come" (John 16:13). How blessed it would be for God's people if they knew no other Counsellor, and sought no other Guide than these which our God has provided!

We would now draw attention to the teaching of the Word of God on the two very important subjects of *the Person and Work of the Holy Spirit,* and *the Authority and Sufficiency of the Holy Scriptures.* Let us take our Bibles and see what God has to say on these important subjects.

The Holy Spirit is the "other Comforter" promised by the Lord Jesus before He left His disciples to go back to heaven (John 14:16). He is a Divine Person and not an "influence" as you might hear Him called by religious people. Think of calling the "eternal Spirit" an "influence"! Ten days after the risen Lord ascended from Mount Olivet and took His seat at the right hand of God, the Holy Spirit came down to earth. From that day until now, He has been here, although, as in the days of the cloudy pillar, the people whose guide He came to be, have proved unfaithful and unworthy of Him. Still He is here, and as our Lord has told us, He will "abide with us for ever" (John 14:16). Not surely because we deserve it, but as during the forty years of wilderness failure and wandering the cloud rested on the blood of atonement on the mercy seat and did not leave them for an hour, so the Holy Spirit abides with us on the ground of redemption accomplished at Calvary.

When a sinner believes the Gospel he is at once *sealed* by the Holy Spirit (Eph 1:13). God puts His seal upon him, and says, "Thou art Mine." The Spirit of God dwells within him, witnessing with his spirit that he is God's child, raising the cry, "Abba, Father" (Gal 4:6). He is the *earnest* of glory to come, and the pledge of the redemption of the body (2 Cor 1:22; Eph 1:14).

Also by this indwelling Spirit, we worship God. God desires our worship, and He deserves it; but only the worship which is produced by the Spirit within the heart of the believer is accepted by the Father (John 4:23-24; Phil 3:3).

He is our *Teacher* (John 16:14; 1 John 2:27). Without His teaching, the Word of God will be a locked treasure; for "the things of God knoweth no man but the Spirit of God" (1 Cor

2:11). This is humbling to man's pride; it sets aside his skill and wisdom and his boasted science. The babe in Christ - the convert of yesterday - in singleness of eye and simplicity of heart, can sit down to search the Word of God with an open mind. As this young believer in Christ depends on the Spirit's teaching, he will learn in reality more of God's truth than all the philosophy of the world can ever teach him. The deep things of God have been hid from the wise and prudent, and revealed to babes (Luke 10:21).

This is comforting to an isolated saint, who may be shut up in some lonely spot, far removed from other believers. The fellowship of saints and the ministry of teachers may be denied him, but he need not despair. He is not left alone. The best of all "expositors" is with him, even the Spirit of God. If he lives in His ungrieved power, the Spirit will open the mysteries of God to his soul; and what he learns thus will not be readily forgotten or let slip. Theoretical knowledge is cheap; it can be picked up with little trouble. It is easily acquired, and as easily let go. But the still small voice of the Spirit, speaking to us in the Word, will cause our hearts to abide in fellowship with God.

Among many of the saints whose principles should surely teach them otherwise, there is often found the idea that only a "learned" man can expound the Scriptures in a way that we can have confidence in, perhaps because he has studied a little of the Greek and Hebrew languages. This leads to the recognition of a false ministry and clerisy, as they exist around us today. The system where clerisy is seen in full bloom, declares that only the ordained pastor or minister or priest can expound the Bible, and the people accept it. Others may not go quite so far as this, but it is dangerous and wrong to believe that God's Word is a sealed book to common people, and that those educated in the world's universities are its only exponents or teachers.

It is our privilege to be *led* by the Spirit, not only in our worship, but also in our walk and every-day life. If we are to enjoy His leading day by day, we must have broken wills and contrite spirits. The Lordship of Christ, His absolute authority over us and the surrender of our wills, must be practically owned in every department of our lives, and His Word alone must give us our instructions. The Spirit's leading will always be contrary to nature and irksome to the flesh. It is a path where faith alone can walk. Remember the path of Jesus. From His baptism in Jordan, He was "led of the Spirit" to be tempted of the devil, and finally to suffer the agony of the Cross.

Are you prepared for such a path, when you ask that God's Spirit may guide you? It means self-denial, trial, and suffering. But be on your guard against a spurious leading of the Spirit, Satan's counterfeit of this blessed reality. Every conceivable ungodly action, done under a pretended sanctity, is attributed to the leading of the Spirit. Believers marry unbelievers, go into partnership in business with them, and sit with them at the communion table, and then tell us they were "led" to do it - "it was laid upon their hearts". This is as false as it is impossible. The Spirit's leading will be always in harmony with, and in no case contrary to, the written Word. The Holy Spirit will always lead the saints to *obey* the Word, never to *ignore* it. How could He inspire an apostle to write, "Be not unequally yoked together with unbelievers" and then lead a believer to disobey it? No path or undertaking can be the leading of the Spirit which has not the sanction of God's written Word. It is an easy thing for the devil to make us believe the Lord is leading us in a certain course, when it is only the will of the flesh to take it. Our safeguard is always to ask ourselves, "Have I been commanded by my Father in heaven to do this? Has He said so in His Word, and where?"

As we thus cleave to the Lord and the Word of His grace, and walk in His Spirit's power, we shall be led on safely. Earth's darkest days shall be lit up with His presence, even though they might be days of sorrow or trial. Our heavenly home is before us, and the way, though rough, is bright. "Blessed is the people that know the joyful sound; they shall walk, O Lord, in the light of Thy countenance" (Psa 89:15).

CHAPTER 11

The Red Sea

There are many believers who do not enjoy settled peace. Sometimes they are bright and happy, at other times sad and downcast ; sometimes their assurance is full and clear, but at other times they are found doubting if they are really saved. Occupied with their thoughts and feelings, their joys and sorrows, they live upon their own experiences. They are looking *in,* instead of having the eye of faith on Christ, looking *up* and rejoicing in Him and the full deliverance from sin and Satan that He has wrought for them.

This may arise from a variety of causes. Some, at the time of their conversion, have only heard and believed an obscure gospel, or part of the gospel of God concerning His Son. They have been taught that to doubt and fear as to their ultimate safety is a certain mark of grace, and that the very best thing that God can find in His saints is an everlasting wail over the evil that dwells within them. Thus they continually live in a hazy atmosphere, brooding over their own experience and attainments, their inward unholiness or corruptions. When we speak about this, we do not want to make believers think lightly of indwelling sin, or underestimate the power of Satan. We believe it is highly important that every saint of God should know the character of the flesh within, and estimate aright the power of the devil against us. But we are equally persuaded that brooding on these things gives no victory over them, and that victory, and not defeat - liberty, and not bondage - is the normal condition of the one who has believed the gospel of God.

The latter part of Romans 7 may be the experience of many; but , we do not believe that it is the everyday experience of a soul which knows death and resurrection with Christ. How could God command His saints to "rejoice evermore" if He gave them no higher note to sing than "O wretched man that I am, who shall deliver me?" (v.24).

These thoughts have been suggested by the position and experience of redeemed Israel, encamped between Migdol and the Sea (Exod 14:2). Pi-hahiroth was their camping ground - it means the "opening of liberty", which to them it truly was. They were still on the borders of Egypt, and within the boundary line of Pharaoh's kingdom. The Red Sea rolled before them and the wilderness had shut them in. Maddened and infuriated at the thought of losing them, Pharaoh with six hundred of his chariots was on their track making a desperate effort to recover his slaves. The people, in fear, cried out to God, for as yet they did not know that He was on their side and against their enemies.

Israel's history at this point tells the experience of many a young believer and describes the state of many a trembling saint of God. Do you see yourself in this?

Perhaps only recently you asked, "What must I do to be saved?" Then your eye was turned to Jesus, as the One who died for sinners, and through faith in Him you had peace with God. But Satan will not let you have peace. Like Pharaoh, he presses hard upon your soul - he brings up the past - he gives you doubts about the future. He tells you that you are his, that you have done his work and must receive his wages. Your state is apparently worse than when you were Christless. You had no such troubles then, for the devil held his goods in peace. Like Israel, you almost wish you had been left in Egypt, quietly doing the devil's work; for it looks as if he will soon have you in his clutches again.

Others around you are happy: they sing for joy, but you can only groan. Possibly they give you very little sympathy, for they do not understand your case. They never were encamped like you, "between Migdol and the Sea". They passed into liberty at once, and in the full sunshine of the gospel of God, they sang their song of deliverance. But no such song is yours, for there is no song in Egypt - no praise "between Migdol and the Sea". The "salvation of the Lord", as typified at the Red Sea, must be known, before the song of deliverance, or the shout of victory can be heard.

The word to Israel was, "*Stand still,* and see the salvation of the Lord, which He will show you to-day, for the Egyptians whom ye have seen to-day, ye shall see no more for ever. The Lord shall fight for you, and ye shall hold your peace" (Exod 14:13-14). And what a word this was for the trembling thousands of Israel! The Lord had undertaken the battle ! He had placed Himself between them and the enemy. It was no longer a question of a battle between Pharaoh and Israel: it was now between Pharaoh and Israel's God. They were to "*stand still and see*". And so it is with us, for Jesus has taken up our cause:

> "*He stood between us and the foe,*
> *And willingly died in our stead.*"

The rod of Moses was stretched out over the sea, and immediately its waters were divided. A pathway was opened through the surging waves, and they stood like crystal walls on either side. This was the Lord's doing, and surely it was marvellous in their eyes.

"Speak to the children of Israel that they *go forward,*" was the next command. "And by faith they passed through the Red Sea" not only where no water was, but on "dry ground" (Heb 11:29). The place of their feet was firm and sure; nothing yielded beneath their step. But it was a path where faith alone could walk, and step by step in faith they trod it, until the other shore was reached.

But then the foe also rushed onward. But alas for the strength of Egypt! - it had entered its final destruction. First, the dark side of the cloud, then the broken chariot wheels, and finally the surging waves of the sea around Pharaoh's mighty host. They were made to feel that Jehovah really fought for Israel and was against their foes. The triumph was complete; not one Egyptian was saved, not a child of Israel was lost. The morning sun shone on an unruffled sea, with Pharaoh's army dead on its shores. The redeemed and delivered captives then stood on its distant shore looking back on the "Salvation of the Lord", and sang their song of victory.

All this is the figure of a mightier conflict, and a grander victory, once won for guilty man. Pharaoh is the type of Satan and Egypt is a type of this world, of which he is the ruler. The Red Sea is the figure of death, the boundary line of Satan's kingdom - his last and greatest stronghold. The camping-ground, "between Migdol and the Sea", is the condition of those who do not as yet know the fullness of the salvation of the Lord, as wrought for them through the death and resurrection of Christ.

Turn for a moment to "the place called Calvary" and to the tomb in the garden which was near it, and contemplate what was done there. Watch the gathering foes and the powers of darkness, and see how each has been met and defeated by the Saviour, and that for ever. This sight will give lasting peace, and if doubts and fears distress you, the Cross will chase them all away.

The *world* was there in every form and grade. The world - religious, political, and profane - was represented around that cross. The world's probation was there closed. Its condemnation was sealed, and its doom written there. By the same blessed work the believer is delivered from this "present evil world", and by the Cross has escaped its doom. As the Red Sea rolled between the children of Israel and Egypt, so the Cross stands between the believer and the world. It is the impregnable barrier that separates us from it for ever.

Do you know this? Do you with your heart believe it - and do you act as if it were true? Do you reckon yourself to have died out of this world with Christ, in order that with Him you might rise to enjoy a better world? Romans 6:4 tells us that our baptism is a symbol of this, and we should be now walking in newness of life with Him.

Satan too was there in all the might of his power. The "Prince of Life" and "him that had the power of death" met on Calvary. It was the decisive contest between the Seed of the woman and the serpent. Satan had the power of death - it was the stronghold of his kingdom. Men of faith, like Hezekiah, wept sore when death drew near. It was untrodden ground, for no one had passed through it and returned to earth again. But Jesus entered the stronghold, and for a time it looked as if He had been conquered. The Prince of Life was laid within the tomb. The stone and seal were put upon Him. The scattered flock and the rejoicing world seemed to say that Satan had gained the day. But his apparent triumph was short. Jesus burst the bars of death. The stone, the watch, and the seal, were all in vain to hold the Prince of Life. "Through death He destroyed him that had the power of death, that is the devil" (Heb 2:14-15). Satan's head was bruised - he was defeated in his own stronghold; his power was broken, and his kingdom conquered.

The Lord is risen indeed! The keys of death are in His hand! He has won for all His people a life beyond death and outwith Satan's power. The weakest saint has life in Christ, even life for evermore. Satan can never capture him again; he is delivered from the power of darkness, and translated into the kingdom of God's dear Son (Col 1:13). Because Christ lives so do we, and through Him we are more than conquerors. The victory is complete. The "Salvation of the Lord" is sure. If you are doubting at this moment, "stand still" just now and behold your victory again. Claim it because it is yours in our Lord Jesus Christ.

CHAPTER 12

The Song of Redemption

"It is a good thing to give thanks unto the Lord" (Psa 92:1); "It is good to sing praises unto our God ; for it is pleasant; and praise is comely" (Psa 147:1). But before we can praise God we must first know Him. To praise an unknown God, or to give thanks to one known only as "hard and austere", demanding and exacting, would be impossible. To ask a mourning heart to sing, or a soul in bondage to praise, would be to mock them. Deliverance must be known and enjoyed - salvation must be accomplished and accepted, before a burst of praise can leave the sinner's lips, or a note of thanksgiving ascend to God. Every question must be settled, the conscience must be at rest, and the heart filled, before praise can begin.

All this is seen in the song of Exodus 15. It is the first recorded song of Scripture; it was sung by a saved people; and the time of their singing was immediately after their salvation. It is good to know all this; for nowadays many sing who should rather weep over their sins and rejection of the gospel; and groans would be a truer expression of their heart than songs. In the previous chapter, this singing company was seen in terror, their enemies around them in power, they cried out in fear, they could not sing. How could they, in the very jaws of threatened death? But now the tables are turned, the foe is routed, and the victory won. The order is, they "*saw*" - they "*believed*" - and then they "*sang*" (Exod 14:31; 15:1). "Then they *believed* His words, they *sang* His praise" (Psa 106:12).

And this is just where praise comes in: it is after salvation, not before it. The feet are first taken up out of "the horrible pit and the miry clay", and then the "new song " fills the mouth (Psa 40:2-3). The prodigal son first received his father's kiss of love; then "they began to be merry". Philip went down to dark Samaria and preached Christ; the people believed the Word, and there was "great joy in that city" (Acts 8:8). The Ethiopian in the desert of Gaza believed, and then "went on his way rejoicing" (Acts 8:39). The story is the same, and so is the order, in every case. Salvation comes first - the joy of salvation and its song follow after.

Can you truthfully take up the language of this song, and say, "He is my God"; "He is become my salvation"? The ungodly can talk of "our Saviour"; and, like the demon-possessed girl at Philippi, they can speak of "the men who show unto us the way of salvation", and yet they remain Christless. But the young convert's first and sweetest song is, "Jesus is mine, and I am His." He can say with David, "The Lord is my rock, and my fortress, and my deliverer; my God, my strength, in whom I will trust; my buckler, and the horn of my salvation, and my high tower" (Psa 18:2). What a constellation of "mys"! It is all so personal ; it is all so sure: no "hoping of being saved"; no thinking it presumption to be sure. It is all assurance here, as in the song on the shore of the Red Sea !

Look, now, at the subject of this "new song". It is all about Jehovah - the glory of His person, the greatness of His power. "The Lord is my strength and song." "The Lord is a man of war." "He hath triumphed gloriously." Not a word about self; not a syllable about what they had done. This is praise. And the new song of heaven shall eternally be, "Worthy is the Lamb". Singing of one's own experience or attainment is not praise; these at best are changeable and imperfect. But Jesus is for ever the same. His glories are unchangeable; and the Father's ear is ever open to hear them told out in His children's praise. Praise is the overflow of a heart filled with a consciousness of God's love and grace; it can only come from someone in the enjoyment of God's salvation.

Crowds of religious men and women may sing psalms and hymns, Sunday after Sunday - there may be the most orthodox language used - the most entrancing music - the most perfect arrangement and harmony - and yet, if they are unsaved, if they have never seen "the salvation of the Lord", if they have not passed through "the Red Sea", the whole affair is a piece of solemn sham. So long as a soul is "dead in trespasses and sins" it cannot praise, for "the dead praise not the Lord" (Psa 115:17). The most daring insults are sometimes offered to the God of heaven under the pretence of praise. The most solemn scenes of Christ's sufferings are set to music, and sung by hundreds of careless sinners, and applauded by thousands more! The death agonies of the Son of God are brought forth in a popular form of song, to please the revolted tastes of wicked men, and dulling their consciences into forgetfulness of the day when the murdered One and the murderers shall meet. The scenes of the "Judgment Day" are turned into lyric, accompanied by strains of music. Many of God's redeemed ones are not clear of this shame, nor are they separate from it. If they would only think of the tenderness of the heart they pierce by this unhallowed work! If they but remembered the depth of the darkness, and the woe that He passed through to make them His, and to separate them from the world that cast Him out, how different all this would appear!

Beloved Christian! we ask you to consider this carefully. We address especially young believers, and we urge upon them the solemn responsibility to stand clear of these works of darkness. We do so because we have seen the feet of the lambs of God's flock led into the snare of the devil through such religious entertainments, when they could not have been by the openly ungodly concert or opera. In the one case it is the devil undisguised, in the other the same devil transformed into an angel of light, and supported by his servants in the garb of "the singers of the house of the Lord" (1 Chron 9:33).

CHAPTER 13

The Wilderness

"So Moses brought Israel from the Red Sea, and they went out into the wilderness of Shur, and they went three days in the wilderness and found no water" (Exod 15:22).

The song, the timbrel, and the dance had just ended, and that first gush of joy and excitement that fills the heart of the newly-delivered ones had subsided. The people now get time to look around and ahead of them on the waste and thirsty desert. Their Canaan home is far in front of them; Egypt is far behind them, and the Red Sea rolls between, to lock them out of it for ever. It is only now that they really begin to find out where they are, and what has happened. They find themselves in a new world, with new surroundings.

The young believer will easily see the application of this to himself. He well remembers the bondage of his former state: then how his eye was turned to look upon the "salvation of the Lord" at the Cross of Jesus, and the empty tomb. What joy and songs of gladness filled his heart ! What hopes and prospects rose before his newborn soul. Everything seemed so changed, the soul was in a new world, earth looked far behind, and heaven so near and real. We all remember those happy hours when we rejoiced in a newly-known Lord Jesus, and it is the will of God we should still be rejoicing "with joy unspeakable and full of glory" (1 Pet 1:8).

However, many speak of these early days of christian life as if they had been mere excitement. They congratulate themselves that now they have settled down to a more sober and intelligent condition. They have gained a deeper knowledge of the Word, and can speak fluently of many things that in earlier days they knew nothing of. That may be it so, but we cannot help thinking that in the case of some, there has been a growth in knowledge without a corresponding enlargement of heart, and if the understanding has gained something, the heart has lost a good deal. There is a want of that warmth of affection and love that marked their earlier days - a love that would have led through flood and flame for Jesus' sake; and even if the energy of nature did at times mingle with it, we believe it was much more pleasing to the Lord, than a clear head and a cold heart will ever be.

Surely a longer acquaintance with the Lord and a deeper knowledge of His ways ought to have the opposite effect. Our affections ought to be the warmer, and our joy the deeper as we go on to know Him. Such joys cannot be the portion of God's new-born sons only, and it should not be that "as we grow older we must grow colder", as some have said. We are sure at least that this is not the will of God, however true it may be in the experience of believers. The excitement may pass away, as does the blossom from the trees, but the precious fruit of the Spirit of God - the love, the joy, the peace (Gal 5:22), will mellow and ripen, as we live in the sunlight and warmth of His presence. "Fulness of joy" (John 15:11; 1 John 1:4), and "continual praise" (Psa 84:4; Heb 13:15) are the blessed portion of all who dwell and walk with God.

But how few continue to go on thus for God, and continue to sing during the discipline of the desert, as they did in the days of youth. How few of the voices that sang the song on the Red Sea shore at the beginning of the wilderness journey, joined in that song of Numbers 21:17, as they neared the end of it! How many had broken down by the way! How many had murmured and had been destroyed! And is it not still the same? I do not speak of the eternal salvation of the soul, but of the failure and declension of those who are saved, on their heavenward journey. Believer, how is it with you? Do you still retain the freshness and simplicity of your first love? Do you find your heart sending forth its streams of praise to God, as it did when first you were converted - it may be years ago? Cold orthodoxy cannot make up for the lack of this. No amount of service done for Him, or knowledge of His Word, is of so great value in the sight of God as the devotedness of a heart full of affection for the person of the Lord Jesus. May we be kept childlike and pure-hearted in the simplicity of true love for Christ.

Coming now to Exodus 15:22 we have an account of the people's first experiences in the wilderness. "They went three days in the wilderness, and found no water." This was trial of a new kind: there had been nothing like this in Egypt. Real wilderness life had now commenced, and they begin to feel the roughness of the way that was leading them to their Canaan home. The Lord who loved them had brought them into the desert to have them alone with Himself (Exod 19:4), that He might lead them and instruct them in many things (Deut 32:10). And this was their first lesson. How unwilling they were to learn it! "The people murmured saying, What shall we drink?" "Hungry and thirsty, their soul fainted in them" (Psa 107:5).

The present world is like this to the children of God: spiritually it is a wilderness. Rightly instructed, they will not seek a portion here, nor expect the comforts of home while on a pilgrim journey. Many dangers will have to be faced, many enemies met, many conflicts endured. Hardships are to be borne - they will "find no water".

Do you not find it like this since you have been converted to God? How changed everything is! Associations and companionships that you loved and enjoyed previous to your conversion have lost their charm and sweetness now. Worldly lusts and pleasures are now foreign to your tastes, as a new creature in Christ. The world is a waste, howling wilderness, and in it you "find no water". There is nothing to refresh or cheer your thirsty soul. But you do not need to murmur or want, for God is the very fountain of life, and He is now teaching you that you must look to Him for satisfaction and sustenance, as well as for salvation.

This is the great lesson of the wilderness - to trust an unseen but present God, to draw from Him day by day, hour by hour, all that you need to sustain you in the desert of this world. This is not learned in a day - nor is it an easy lesson. But we need not fear, for we know the hand that is leading us on, and the love of the heart that is planning for us. Should He lead us through seas of trouble, where our spirit is overwhelmed, and our tears flow, we know He will not leave us. Rather as He draws each false and failing prop from under us, on which He sees we may lean too fondly, it is so that He may draw us the closer to Himself, to prove how good and kind He is. Thus chastened, subdued, and weaned away from trusting in an arm of flesh, we will go along the wilderness leaning on the arm of our Beloved Lord.

At **Marah** there is a yet deeper trial. "And when they came to Marah they could not drink of the waters of Marah, for they were bitter" (Exod 15:23). What at first sight seemed able to give relief, was found to be only bitterness. Do our hearts cling to something of earth, rather than trust the living God, and let Him provide? But He loves us too well to allow this, and so He turns our fancied joys to bitterness. We have all had our Marahs to pass since first we began our christian life. Some have found them at home, others in the world. It has been truly bitter for some to find a once-fond parent turned against them for Jesus' sake, or to be looked upon with contempt and scorn by those we once hoped would have helped us. To bear the daily frown of a cold and cruel world, and to be looked upon with suspicion by those we seek to help is bitter enough to nature. But we need not be surprised at all this, for it is only what He promised, and we are only in company with the Master Himself, and the saints of former days. He told us that in the world we should have tribulation, and that through tribulation we should enter the kingdom (John 16:33; Acts 14:22). Although some who profess to be the Lord's have found out an easy way to heaven, in which they can have the world's friendship and approval, the old road, where Jesus and His suffering saints have trod, has its Marahs still, and who would be such a coward as to shrink from it?

Look at Paul. Converted on his way to persecute the suffering saints of God, he was immediately told how great things he must suffer for Jesus' sake (Acts 9:16), and what these sufferings were, let 2 Corinthians 11:23-28 tell. The first Epistle of Peter, which especially views the believer as a pilgrim passing through the desert, has for its keynote the word "suffer". Look at 2:19; 3:14-17; 4:12-19: what a record of suffering, but what consolations too!

At Marah, the Lord showed Moses a tree, which, when he had thrown into the waters, made them sweet. How near to the waters of bitterness was the tree of sweetness found! How close to the suffering pilgrim of 1 Peter is the suffering Son of God. Read the words of 2:21-23; 3:17,18; 4:13, and you will find the tree is in the waters, so that they are made sweet. We are treading the same desert that His dear feet once trod. We meet the same kind of trials as He met, and who would fear to tread a path where we have such fellowship with Him? The dreadful and bitter cup of the wrath of God He drank Himself alone; that kind of suffering we can never share. But the suffering that came to Him for righteousness' sake, and as God's witness in an evil world, is the suffering that we may share; and we shall, if we walk with Him along this path. Others shared it who have gone before. Look at Paul and Silas in the prison at Philippi; first cruelly treated, then their feet made fast in the stocks. This was Marah, but the tree was in the waters. Praises rang through the prison that night, and we know what followed. The Marah waters were made sweet.

See the three Hebrew young men cast into that raging furnace in Babylon. Noble witnesses they were for the truth of the God they loved! But they were not left to walk alone in the furnace: they got a companion to walk with them whose "form was like the Son of God"; and who would object to walk, even there, in such company?

The lesson to be learned by us is this - that it is not the Lord's way to remove the prison, or to extinguish the fires, but rather to be very near us while we endure them. He does not promise to keep us exempt from the trial, but He has promised to be with us in it, and "with the temptation also to make a way of escape that we may be able to bear it" (1 Cor 10:13). This applies to hundreds of the smaller things of everyday life. He does not remove the "thorn", but gives "grace" to bear it (2 Cor 12:8,9), and thus the bitterness is made sweet. So "we glory in tribulations also" (Rom 5:3).

Elim, with its twelve wells and seventy palm trees, comes next: a green spot in the desert, and all the more enjoyable after the trial. Elim was not Canaan, but it was a refreshing spot on the way, and a happy foretaste of the time when Israel would dwell in the land, and keep the feast of tabernacles under the shade of the palm tree. When our wilderness days are past, we shall enter into the glory of heaven, of which we even now have the earnest and the hope. We grasp this "blessed hope", and long for the joys of home, when we have just been at the bitter waters; for "trials make the promise sweet".

The wells of divine promise are deep and exhaustless. The "sufferings" and the "glory" are closely linked together in 1 Pet 1:11; 4:13; 5:1,10. Even here our Marahs and Elims are very near each other. The little crew on the lake of Galilee must have enjoyed the calm He gave them, after so wild a storm! How the hearts of Martha and Mary must have overflowed with joy at the feast of reunion in John 12, after the sorrow and tears of separation in John 11. And thus it shall be with us, when He finally hushes the storms of life to rest, and together with our loved ones raised, He receives us to our eternal home. Oh how grand it will be to be there!

"There, beside life's crystal river,
There, beneath life's wondrous tree,
There, with nought to cloud or sever,
Ever with the Lamb to be,
Heir of Glory! what a hope for you and me!"

CHAPTER 14

The Manna

The manna was the food of the children of Israel in the wilderness. For forty long years it was given to them morning by morning, from the hand of their faithful God. Neither their murmurings nor their sins restrained Him from sending it, until their feet stood in the land of their possession, and they had eaten of its fruit. "Then the manna ceased after they had eaten of the old corn of the land; neither had the children of Israel manna any more" (Josh 5:12).

We may gather very precious and practical lessons from the manna. Like Israel in the wilderness, we are hungry. The new life within us, begotten of God, finds no sustenance in this present evil world. It sighs for heavenly things, it hungers after God. Worldly things are foreign to the taste of the "new man", although "the flesh", still lurking in the believer, can relish them well. Let us be on our guard then and watch, lest we feed the old and starve the new. It is the new which should be fed - on manna from heaven.

Exodus 16 opens with a view of the wilderness, and a murmuring camp of people complaining for want of bread. It is the second month since Egypt was left behind, and whatever bread they had brought in their kneading troughs was exhausted. There was no help for them except from God; and, blessed be His Name, He was near and ready to take the responsibility of supplying all their needs. Not surely because they deserved it, for the sequel shows the reverse, but because He loved them with a love which all their murmurings could not quench. Blessed it was for them that such a love is His, and blessed it is for us. He provided for them according to His love for them. And so the manna fell in rich abundance from the courts of heaven, right down at their very doors. Unearned by the sweat of their brow, it fell during the hours of night while they slept, the gift of God, and they had only to gather it and eat. "Man did eat angels' food" - "He *satisfied* them with the bread of heaven" (Psa 78:25; 105:40).

The Lord Jesus is the manna for our souls; it is by feeding on Him that our spiritual life is nourished and sustained. As only He can give life, so only He can sustain it. And He does this by presenting Himself to us in the written Word by the Holy Spirit. It is not only in His death as the Lamb slain, nor only in His resurrection from the dead, as the old corn of Canaan; but also as the One who humbled Himself, who was here in this world in the likeness of men - the Word made flesh who dwelt among us. As strangers here, we need the friendship and the consolation of One who has been Himself a stranger here, and this we have in Jesus. How cheering to our souls it is to trace His footsteps from the manger to the Cross, as recorded in the Gospels. The manna character of Jesus appears there: the small, round thing, lying on the face of the wilderness, unknown and unnamed among men. He came in the night of the world's darkness, and passed away unheeded and despised by those He came to bless. The Jewish nation knew Him not (John 1:11), but His people know Him, and delight to feed upon Him as the One who humbled Himself.

The manna was *white*. It lay unsullied in the dewdrop on the sand of the desert. Such was the blessed Lord. Although in the world, and continually moving amongst its defiling scenes, He was holy, harmless, and undefiled: white in His unsullied path from the manger to the Cross, even as His garments were on that transfiguration mount.

Just as the incarnate Word is pure, clean and perfect, so is the written Word that reveals Him. Infidelity and superstition have done their best to prove there are spots and imperfections in it, but they have failed. The Word shines on in its brightness, and the saints confidently and adoringly proclaim, "Thy Word is very pure: therefore thy servant loveth it" (Psa 119:140).

The manna was *sweet* - the taste was like honey. The Philistines once asked, "What is sweeter than honey?" The youngest saint can answer, "How sweet are Thy words unto my taste! yea, sweeter than honey to my mouth" (Psa 119:103).

Such is the bread on which the Lord would have us feed during our pilgrimage here. Even after life's journey is past, we shall surely not forget the bread of our wilderness days; for an omer was to be treasured for a memorial in the inner sanctuary (Exod 16:33). The manna once lying on the desert, was lifted up and treasured in the "golden pot" within the vail (Heb 9:4). The gold here, as elsewhere, speaks of glory. Jesus who had nowhere to lay His head on earth, is glorified in the highest heaven, and we shall behold His glory. But even then, the memory of His humiliation shall not be forgotten. We shall never forget Gethsemane and Golgotha. The memories of Bethany and Nain shall be with us, and we shall "eat of the hidden manna" (Rev 2:17) in its everlasting sweetness there.

The manner in which the manna was gathered is of great importance to us: *"They gathered every man according to his eating"*. God gave it; they gathered it. It had to be appropriated by them in order to be enjoyed. And so it must be with us. There is bread enough and to spare, there is fulness in Christ for all our needs, but we must diligently gather it up from the Word for ourselves. No believer can expect to prosper in soul, if he or she neglects the Word of God. It is the means appointed by God, by which He ministers strength and sustenance to His people. The one who slights or overlooks this will be a great loser. If a man neglects to feed his body, his strength will soon diminish, and his whole constitution will suffer! So it is with the inner man, the soul, though not many perceive this.

Dear Christian! can we press this matter home upon your heart and conscience? It is a matter of immense importance and one affecting the very vitals of Christianity. The low state of spiritual life among the people of God, the lack of divine power in the service of the Lord, and the sadly inconsistent walk of many who profess to be the Lord's, are things deplored and mourned over among us. But is there not a cause? Undoubtedly there is; and we would humbly suggest that the chief cause is this - neglect of the soul's nourishment, *through a lack of meditation on the Word, alone with God.* This is a busy age. Things go at a great speed, and everything tends to draw the saints from their quiet times with God and their Bibles. Controversies in the church, and upheavals in the world are engrossing the attention of many of the saints, and the devil is making capital of the occasion by quietly alluring saints from the solace of the "secret place". Troubles and perplexities exist in the commercial world, and from early till late, Christians are occupied planning how those difficulties are to be met. It is perfectly right that Christians should have their business so ordered that the world will not be able to point the accusing finger at any inconsistency in it, but nothing on earth can justify the habitual neglect of communion with God in meditation on His Word, nor will God's blessing rest upon anyone who neglects this. It may be that such times with God will by necessity be short, but the Lord knows all our circumstances, and He can make a little gathering go a long way, "for he that gathered little had no lack". Every man gathered according to his eating, some more, some less, but the manna was adapted to the requirements of each; so little children, young men, and fathers, each can find their own portion in the Word (1 John 2:12-17).

The next point is - *it was gathered early.* The camp was early on the move. Gathering manna was their morning work, for "when the sun waxed hot it melted". This is an important point. "They that seek Me early shall find Me", is a statute in the kingdom of God, and in the experience of the saints. "He wakeneth morning by morning, He wakeneth mine ear to hear" (Isa 50:4), was the language of the perfect Man. It was His custom "a great while before day", to seek the "solitary place" alone with God (Mark 1:35). The early dew was often brushed from the grass by His feet, as He went to the mountain-side to commune secretly with His God.

The early-gathered manna is the sweetest. If the daily newspaper or the morning's letters are the first thing you seek each day, there will be only a feeble appetite for the heavenly manna. If household cares or business anxieties are allowed to crowd in upon your soul before it has received strength from God through meditation on His Word, it is no wonder if things become a drag and burden all day. Someone has written, "If I neglect morning meditation on the Word and prayer, nothing goes well during the day." Of course where the blessedness of the early-gathered manna has never been enjoyed, the lack of it cannot be felt. But strengthened by the bread of God, renewed in the inner man morning by morning, we can go out calmly to meet the demands of life, courageously encounter its conflicts, and steadfastly bear its daily cross. Whilst many of God's people have very little time to meditate on the Word because of the nature of their working lives, the Lord is not ignorant of our circumstances, and He can give much strength out of the little that has been diligently gathered.

Now we note that *it was gathered daily*. Yesterday's portion will not do for to-day. Lord's Day's manna will not suffice for Monday. It had to be gathered fresh and used, or else it bred worms and stank. Truth stored in the notebook or just in the intellect, unexperienced by the soul and unpractised in the walk, is of little value: it neither sanctifies nor nourishes. Retailing out to others what has never been experienced by ourselves, cannot be a blessing. It only "stinks" in people's nostrils, and puffs up ourselves. It is "by reason of use" that we grow in the knowledge of Christ. Practising what we know, God gives us more. As we walk uprightly in the ways of God along the desert road, we shall never lack an appetite for the heavenly manna which will always be available till the wilderness is past.

We also find in Numbers 11 that *the Manna was despised.* What a change! How soon the fine gold grows dim, and the warmth of first love declines. The second year of desert life often finds the saints of God less true-hearted than the first. So it was with Israel. Redemption by blood, deliverance from Egypt, and even the daily manna had become insipid things to them now, very commonplace to hearts that had departed from the living God. The truth is, "in their hearts they had turned back to Egypt" (Acts 7:39), and now they remember the good things they once had there, and sigh to obtain them. They remembered Egypt's dainties and delicacies, but not the brickmaking and the hard bondage. The devil takes good care not to remind them of their former state; but he holds up the pleasures of it to the best advantage, and the result is God's manna is despised.

Do you know anything of this fellow-believer? Can you honestly say, *"Jesus, Thou art enough",* as you did when first converted? You remember those happy days when He was so precious, and the Word of God was so sweet that told you of Him. How eagerly you read and searched the Scriptures, and seized each spare moment to do so. Your Bible was your constant companion; worldly magazines, novels, and light literature had no attraction then. Jesus, and "Jesus only", was enough. There was pleasure in Him, recreation enough in His service; nothing more was wanted. Do you find it so to-day? Alas, many do not. They have, like Israel of old, turned back in heart to Egypt, and desired its pleasures. What they cast aside long ago is now keenly pursued. Things they once gave up, as unworthy of Christ, are now their boast.

What about worldly gatherings, the so-called innocent amusements, the questionable songs listened to and sung by many, and yet a conspicuous absence from the prayer-meeting? The well-thumbed novel and the dust-covered Bible, the hours spent in trifling conversation and the minutes in prayer, tell their own story. As an excuse for this some will say, "We cannot be always speaking about Christ; we cannot be always reading our Bible ; we must have some change, some variety." This is just the old story of Numbers 11:6 - "There is nothing at all beside this manna." What more "beside" is needed? Is Jesus not enough to satisfy? The everlasting song of heaven will be Jesus, only Jesus; and if He will be enough for heaven, why not for earth? If enough for eternity, why not for time?

The "mixed multitude" were the first to lust after Egypt's food, and the rest followed. So beware of people with a religious profession, or even Christians of mixed principles and carnal ways. They can often do more to lead young believers away from God than an open enemy.

But this is not all. This lusting after Egypt's food changed for them the taste of the manna. Once it was "like honey", now it is said to be like "fresh oil". Anyone knows the difference: the sweetness had gone. And not satisfied with the manna as it came, they began to bake it into cakes, perhaps to save the trouble of gathering it daily. When the heart gets away from God, how little sweetness has the Word. It becomes a barren and tasteless chore to read through a single chapter. Manna cakes are easier found. Explanations of the Word, and sermons or addresses from the Word, mixed with man's ideas, suit the taste better, and a lot of trouble is saved by reading these instead of the Word! The soul that prefers man's words about Christ, to God's own testimony concerning His Son, is in a bad way.

Numbers 21 shows how this evil develops. The people tell God, "There is no bread . . . and our soul loatheth this light bread." Judgement followed these fearful words. How often has back-sliding begun in the heart, prayer and meditation on the Word has been neglected, and it is soon followed by an open fall. It may even require the discipline of God's rod to awaken the sluggish soul out of the devil's snare. How much more pleasing to God, and joyful for us, when the heart can truly sing-

> *"Jesus, Thou art enough*
> *The mind and heart to fill."*

CHAPTER 15

The Smitten Rock

"My soul thirsteth for God, for the living God" (Psa 42:2). "O God, Thou art my God; early will I seek Thee: my soul thirsteth for Thee, my flesh longeth for Thee in a dry and thirsty land, where no water is" (Psa 63:1). These are the breathings of a child of God in the wilderness; the expression of that divine and heavenly life which has its source and supply in the living God.

It may be truly said of this life that it came from God, and goes to God. Like water rising to its own level, its aspirations reach up to the God from whom it came, and nothing short of this will give true satisfaction to the "new man" in the believer. Dead forms and ceremonies of religion may satisfy people who have no real spiritual life in them, but the truly heaven-born soul will, as the thirsty hart pants after the waterbrooks, long for direct, personal dealing with the living God. It will break through each rank of the opposing powers of darkness, until it gains its object. This will be true in some measure in every child of God. It is one of the distinguishing marks between the man of the world and the child of God, between those who have the Christ-life within them, and those who are dead in sin.

As we read the opening verses of Exodus 17, we see the camp of Israel in a barren desert without a drop of water. What will they do this time? They murmur again, and speak angrily to Moses. It was unbelief that led them to complain, for their eye was off Jehovah, their God, and yet their very failure was a proof that they were out of Egypt and in the desert with God. We never read of Egyptians complaining like this, nor did the children of Israel do so as long as they sat by the river of Egypt. But now they are in the place of need, where faith is tried, and where, alas it so often fails. In spite of all their murmurings, the Lord was right at hand, and ready to satisfy that thirsty camp with water, as He had satisfied the hungry camp with manna in chapter 16. This is what we too have often found since we began our desert life as saints of God.

Moses was commanded to take the rod with which he had turned the river of Egypt into blood, and smite the rock in Horeb. When this was done, the water gushed forth. The very rod, whose stroke was judgement to the Egyptians, was used in grace to bring the refreshing streams of water to the many thousands of thirsty Israelites.

The spiritual meaning of this to us is very plain, as taught in 1 Corinthians 10:4 - "that rock was Christ": Christ smitten in judgement on the Cross for our blessing. The water is the type of the Holy Spirit given to us, as the fruit of Christ's death and His completed work. Had the rock not been smitten, the stream would have been closed up inside it; and had the blessed Lord not borne the heavy stroke of judgement for us, there could have been no salvation and no giving of the Spirit of God. But blessed be His peerless Name, He who was once "stricken, smitten of God, and afflicted", has now gone up to be glorified in the highest heaven. The Spirit has come down as the witness of His exaltation, and of the purging of our sins (John 7:39 ; Heb 10:15); and He dwells in all believers as the strengthener and sustainer of their spiritual being.

Of Israel we read, "they did *all* drink the same spiritual drink" (1 Cor 10:4); and of believers now, that they have been "*all* made to drink into one Spirit" (1 Cor 12:13). This is the birthright and the heritage of every member of the family of God. There is no such thing as a believer in Christ who has not received the Spirit. There are some who deny this, and try to teach that certain of the people of God have not received the seal of the Holy Spirit. But this is opposed to the teaching of the Scripture. What we learn there, is that "as many as received Him (Christ), to them gave He power to become the children of God" (John 1:12) ; and "because ye are sons, God hath sent forth the Spirit of His Son into your hearts, crying, Abba, Father" (Gal 4:6). It is not because you know this or that doctrine, or because you have attained to this measure of devotedness, or to that of holiness, but "because ye are sons", and "ye are all sons of God through faith in Christ Jesus" (Gal 3:26). "The Spirit Himself beareth witness with our spirit that we are the children of God (Rom 8:16); and "if any man have not the Spirit of Christ, he is none of His" (Rom 8:9).

But we must distinguish between things that differ. There is a great difference between believers having received the Spirit, and "being filled with the Spirit" (see 1 Cor 2:12, with Eph 5:18). There is also a distinction made between life and growth. The life is the same in all believers, but the development of that life may be different in each one. The Spirit of God dwells in every child of God, but the evidences of that may be greater or lesser. The new-born babe has life in Christ, and there is no other life. Such terms as the "Higher Life", the "Holy Life", are misnomers and unscriptural. The life is of the same character in all, although it may vary in development and manifestation in each. The Scriptures speak of the "weak" and the "strong" (Rom 15:1); the "carnal" and the "spiritual" (1 Cor 3:1); but here it is a question of development and not of the character of the life received. Some, because of worldliness and false teaching, like the Corinthian and Galatian saints, are going back; and others, like the Thessalonians, are "growing exceedingly" and abounding in the graces of the Spirit. Stephen and Barnabas were men "full of the Holy Ghost" (Acts 7:55; 11:24); while some at Corinth were only "babes", envying and striving with one another (1 Cor 3:1-3), yet even they are addressed as "sanctified in Christ Jesus, called saints" - their bodies the temple of the Holy Ghost (1 Cor 1:2; 6:13).

We all know the difference between the tiny stream, and the mighty river overflowing its banks, although the water is the same in both. May it be ours to "be filled with the Spirit" (Eph 5:18), and to walk in the Spirit (Gal 5:16). This is what our God has commanded us, and those who, through grace, know most of the blessed experience of this, will have the least to say about it. Like Moses, when he descended from the mount with the skin of his face shining, it will be evident to all, and we shall not require to tell it; it will tell itself. The weary and thirsty souls we come in contact with, will get the benefit of it, for if we are drinking deep at the fountain ourselves, the living waters will flow out of us in "rivers" (John 7:37- 38). This is the great need of the present hour among all who teach the Word among the saints, and preach the Gospel to the world around. The Lord preserve us from being satisfied with sound and orthodox preaching, devoid of the life-giving power of the Spirit of God. To walk with God and serve Him in this way, we need to give heed to the weighty admonitions of Scripture: "Grieve not the Holy Spirit of God" (Eph 4:30), "Quench not the Spirit" (1 Thess 5:19).   Alas we often do so, and this is the cause of much of our weakness and barrenness.

In Numbers 20:7-11, we get further mention made of the rock. Here Moses is commanded to *"speak* to the rock, and it shall give forth its water". There was to be no second smiting; it was smitten once for all, and now the word was - "Speak to the rock." But Moses spoke to the people - unadvisedly too - and *smote* the rock. He disobeyed God, and for this he was not allowed to enter the land of Canaan as Israel's leader.

Our Rock, Christ Jesus, has been once smitten upon the cross, and as the result, the Spirit has been given. We do not need to ask the Holy Spirit to come down, or plead with God to send Him down to dwell in us. He is in us already, as the witness of the perfect purgation of our sins (Heb 10:15), as the seal of our present redemption, and as the earnest of our future glory (Eph 1:13-14). In the same way as a well in a garden supplies moisture to the plants, and as the stream flowing through the fields causes the seed to spring and grow, and bear its fruit, so is the Spirit of God in the believer. He who draws near to God, and "speaks to the Rock", will lack no moisture; his leaf will be green and, like the palm tree, he will be full of sap and flourishing. The words he speaks will refresh the weary saints, and from him the stream of life shall flow to needy sinners all around. His soul shall be "like a watered garden, and like a spring of waters whose waters fail not".

How we should long to know the fullness of the Spirit of God; to drink deep of the stream that produces health and fruit; and at the same time avoid whatever would lure us away from the smitten side of Him with whom is "the fountain of life", to the "broken cisterns" of the world which cannot satisfy.

CHAPTER 16

War with Amalek

In Exodus 17:8-16 we read about the children of Israel
meeting their first enemy and fighting their first battle as the
Lord's redeemed people. From the first gathering of the
manna, and the first refreshment from the stream that flowed
from the smitten rock, Israel now passes on to different
scenes. They would willingly have gone on in peace to
Canaan - they did not ask for war; they were not the
aggressors. Amalek, a near kinsman of Israel's according to
the flesh, a grandson of Esau, has now increased into a strong,
warlike people - "the first of the nations" (Num 24:20) and
has come forth to impede the progress of Israel, and to fight
against them in the desert.

Notice that this unprovoked attack came from Amalek,
not from Israel. Its objective was to exterminate the people
of the Lord, to blot them out. It was cunningly done, for we
read, "He laid wait for him in the way" (1 Sam 15:2). It was
cowardly too, for the "feeble", the "faint and weary", were
set upon first; and the "hindmost" of the people were also
attacked. There are many lessons here for our souls.
Remember again that "the things that were written aforetime
were written for our learning", in order that we may be
equipped for our spiritual warfare of which this is a type.

The enmity of Amalek against Israel was nothing new. It
was only the continuation of the old struggle between the
elder and the younger - the child of flesh and the child of
promise. This was seen in Ishmael as he persecuted Isaac;
in Esau as he struggled with Jacob from the hour of his birth

81

and onward; and now in Amalek against the new-born nation, redeemed and separated to be Jehovah's chosen people.

So long as the people of Israel were in slavery in Egypt they had no fighting to do. Amalek stayed in his place, and his enmity was unnoticed. But no sooner have redemption and separation to God been accomplished, the manna tasted and the water drunk, than he comes forward to oppose and fight. So we learn that Amalek is the enemy of a redeemed and pilgrim people, that this warfare is unknown in days of slavery; and that deliverance from Pharaoh therefore precedes war with Amalek.

The answer to this in the experience of the children of God is both striking and instructive. Amalek, which means "a people that licks up", is the type of the flesh within us. The war in Rephidim with Israel, is a type of that conflict known only to those who have been redeemed to God, delivered from the authority of darkness, and separated from this present evil world. Unconverted people know nothing of it; they are under the dominion of the flesh, they serve its lusts and they do its will. It does not therefore fight its subjects; it rules over them. But from the moment of the second birth, and the indwelling of the Holy Spirit, the conflict with the flesh begins. And as it was in the type, so it is in reality - the flesh begins the struggle. The new-born soul, alive to God and pressing on along the heavenly path, would feed on the manna (Christ), and drink of the water from the rock (the Spirit) in peace; but the flesh will not allow it. We read that "the flesh lusteth against the Spirit" (Gal 5:17).

The first attack of this subtle enemy is often a surprise to the young believer. He has just begun his wilderness journey with a song; the fetters of his sin have been broken; he has eaten of the heavenly bread, and drunk of the refreshing water. The sins and the sorrows of his former life are past, and he has lost taste for things that once charmed him in the world. Were it not for the thorns that surround his path, he would almost forget that "this world is a wilderness wide", so great is his joy, and so satisfied his soul, as he walks along calmly with his God.

But suddenly the enemy is met, and the conflict begins in earnest. Some old habit has asserted its power; some evil suggestion darts into his thoughts; some fleshly lust demands to be indulged. The effect on the young believer is appalling. He never counted on this; he thought the days for such things were past. A new creature in Christ, and a son of God, indwelt by the Holy Spirit, he imagined that the flesh within him had either died, or ceased to be. So quiet and inoffensive had it been since the time of his conversion, that he imagined (and some have even said this) that it had been eradicated, root and branch. But, alas ! it was not so. Seductive, treacherous, and subtle, it only lay in ambush watching its chance to attack the heaven-born life, the new man created in righteousness, and to war against the Spirit of God now dwelling within the child of faith.

The flesh and the Spirit are distinct and essentially different, just as Amalek and Israel were in the desert. The Spirit of God neither eradicates nor absorbs the flesh in a believer. The flesh may not be expelled; it cannot be improved. It is evil, only evil, always evil; enmity against God. We are told by God to have "no confidence" in it (Phil 3:2); to make "no provision" for it (Rom 13:14); not to "yield our members" as weapons to its service (Rom 6:13). It will always oppose, but it need not oppress; it will ever be in conflict, but it need never conquer; for the Lord of Hosts, mighty in battle, is on our side, and He gives us the victory.

Israel was no match for the foe that here confronted them. Amalek was "the first of the nations", a people accustomed to warfare. Israel had "seen no war" (Exod 13:17), and had no experience in handling the sword and shield. Had the battle been joined on the basis of human strength, the result would doubtless have been the defeat of Israel. But God in high heaven could not allow this. The infant nation was weak and unfit for conflict, but they were the people of Jehovah. They had been redeemed and separated unto Him. His arm had been strong for their deliverance from Pharaoh, and He will not now stand silently by and see them overthrown by Amalek. His power had been exercised for them in the defeat of Pharaoh's army; that same power is now to be exercised through them for the victory over Amalek.

The lesson here is of great encouragement to us as the redeemed of the Lord. There are times when it seems as if we are going to be swallowed up quickly, and our enemies might easily triumph over us. If it was left to us, this might easily happen. Sin in the flesh is a strong and relentless enemy; it has had long experience, and finds in the young believer one who appears to be an easy prey. But the Lord of Hosts is for us. Divine power is on our side. The power that once was so evident in raising Christ from among the dead, now works in the feeblest saint (Eph 1:19; 3:20), and that power is our strength in our battles. Thank God, the ultimate victory is sure. For a time it may seem as if "Amalek prevails", but his latter end is "that he perish for ever" (Num 24:20).

The manner in which this victory was won, has very important lessons for the children of God. The battlefield had its upper and lower spheres. Up on the hilltop, Moses held the rod - the symbol of Jehovah's power. Down in the valley Joshua used the sword upon "the strength of Amalek". So long as Moses' hands held up the rod, Joshua's victory with the sword was assured; but when these hands fell down, the victory passed to Amalek. Moses on the hill is a type of the believer in communion with God. While he abides there, his hands uplifted in conscious need, the power of God is exercised on his behalf. "When I am weak then am I strong" is the experience of a saint on the hill, with the rod of God in his hand. But it is not possible for man to abide in this position by himself: he must be helped to maintain it, or else his hands will soon hang feebly down. So Aaron (exalted) and Hur (freeborn) take their places by his side, and by them his hands are upheld, until the battle has been fought and the victory won, by the sword of Joshua.

This is at least an illustration of the two advocates or helpers, given to us as believers, by whom our communion and strength can be sustained in wilderness warfare. We have on the one side a great High Priest within the veil, who ever lives to make intercession for us there (Heb 7:25), an advocate with the Father, Jesus Christ the Righteous (1 John 2:2). Our cause is well represented there, by the One whose word to all His people is, "I will strengthen thee; yea, I will help thee; yea, I will uphold thee by the right hand of My righteousness" (Isaiah 41:11). On the other side we have the Holy Spirit, the "other Comforter"(or "advocate" - the word is the same as in 1 John 2:2) of whom it is written, "In like manner the Spirit also helpeth our infirmities: the Spirit Himself maketh intercession for us" (Rom 8:26). Thus, having one Intercessor for us *with* God, and another Intercessor *in* us from God, the believer has power to prevail. We need never be defeated by the flesh although it will keep on trying to defeat us.

But there is another aspect to this warfare. Joshua, handling the sword against Amalek, shows the believer using the sharp two-edged sword of the Word of God (Heb 4:12) against his own flesh, mortifying (or making dead) its "lusts" (Col 3:5), "casting down" its "reasonings" (2 Cor 10:5) and no longer minding its "things" (Rom 8:5). This warfare is not imaginary, but real; and the one who dwells habitually on the hill with God, will know best how fierce is the battle in the valley with the flesh which is, and always will be, at enmity with God. Do not be misled by sentimental and one-sided theories of a "rest of faith", where no war is known; or of a peaceful region where no enemy like Amalek may come. Sometimes the language of poetry speaks of such a place, but the warrior of the wilderness remembers the word uttered at the end of that day of battle; "The Lord will have war with Arnalek from generation to generation" (Exod 17:16), and keeps his sword ever ready by his side.

In later days, we read of Amalek reappearing as the enemy

of Israel. Agag the Amalekite king was spared by Saul, and the best of the sheep and oxen were reserved under the plea of doing sacrifice to the Lord (1 Sam 15:9-15). Because of this, Saul was rejected and lost the kingdom, and it is salutary to note that he who spared that Amalekite from the sword of the Lord, was killed at last himself by the hand of an Amalekite (2 Sam 1:10,13). A man of a different spirit was Mordecai the Jew, who refused to bow to, or acknowledge Haman the Agagite as his overlord. Although Haman was in a place of favour with the king, Mordecai discerned this haughty man to be an oppressor of Israel, and the enemy of the Lord (Esther 3:1-6). At that critical time in Israel's history, as it has ever been and ever will be, obedience to God gained the day. Israel, as represented in Mordecai, even though an exile in a strange land, honoured God and prevailed, and Amalek, in the person of the haughty Agagite, was overthrown in shame.

CHAPTER 17

An Interlude before Sinai

When we reach Exodus 19, we will notice that a new phase in the experience of the Israelites begins, as they go on through the wilderness. They are about to receive God's holy law, and become His covenanted people. They will prepare to make for Him a tabernacle to dwell in the midst of them, and they will be able to worship Him in the wilderness according to His revealed pattern. This was one of the reasons for their deliverance from Egypt, as we noticed earlier.

But before that, in chapter 18, after the battle and the victory at Rephidim, some interesting scenes are described for us. It is a sort of interlude on the journey, as we read about some family matters of Moses, the leader himself. After a period of separation from them, he is met by his wife Zipporah, their sons Gershom and Eliezer, and his father in law Jethro.

Looked at typically, it gives us a beautiful picture of the one thousand year rule of our Lord Jesus Christ over the whole earth, as prophesied in the Scriptures. This reign is often referred to by Bible students as 'the Millennium'. You can read about it in passages such as Rev 20:1-7, Psa 2:6-12, and many parts of the prophecies of Isaiah and Zechariah describe its glorious conditions. When our Lord Jesus came into the world the first time, He was rejected, despised, and shamefully crucified. But when He comes again, He will first take out of the world His church, composed of believers who have died or are alive at the time, then a little later He will appear in power and great glory to set up His kingdom on earth. He will rule as King of kings and Lord of lords, Jerusalem will be His royal city, and all nations will honour and obey Him. Read Psalm 72 for a description of this wonderful reign.

So in Exodus 18 we have the Gentile nations, as represented in Jethro, a foreigner from Midian, rejoicing in Jehovah's goodness to Israel. He acknowledges the goodness and greatness of God (vv.9-11), as the nations of the world will do in that great time of blessing for all. Also the tribes of Israel are here, with much travail and sorrow behind them, representing that nation in those days to come, after the fiery trial of their "great tribulation" is past, gathered in peace under their Messiah-King. Then in Zipporah and her sons, we see the Church, the Bride of Christ, and many sons brought to glory (Heb 2:10). In the latter half of the chapter we have a picture of perfect administration such as will mark the millennial reign of Christ, when no cause will be overlooked, no injustice permitted, and no problem unsolved.

However, as elsewhere in the wilderness journey, here we get only a brief glimpse of coming glory, a passing gleam of sunshine in a cloudy day. The "way of the wilderness", with its remaining toils and conflicts, has again to be faced and covered, and so they will come to the desert of Sinai, and encamp before the mount of God.

Great events are about to happen there, and lessons learned by the pilgrim nation, which will never be forgotten. Such experiences are necessary in the life history of God's people today. Individually and collectively we must encamp, stay still in quietness, and listen to the Voice that speaks to us. Service and conflict must be laid aside, and often in solitudes greater than Horeb, the word of law and grace will come with power to the souls of the people of the Lord. Yet it does not need to come with alarm, for well we know - in a way that Israel did not know - that He who speaks, speaks not in wrath, but speaks as a Father to His children, and only for their best blessing and their deeper joy.

CHAPTER 18

Giving the Law

The giving of the law is the first of the great events recorded during the encampment at Sinai. To Israel, this was the beginning of a new dispensation in God's ways of dealing with them. Up till now His grace had always worked for them: their sins and murmurings had only brought forth fresh provisions from His gracious hand. Till now blessing had been given to them unconditionally, and in spite of their failure. Jehovah's heart and hand had been toward them, fulfilling the promise made in a covenant with their father Abraham (Gen 15:13-14). "Ye have seen what I did unto the Egyptians and how I bare you on eagle's wings, and brought you unto Myself" (Exod 19:4), are words that tenderly describe the character of Jehovah's dealings with His people.

But now the blessing is to be continued on the ground of their obedience: "If ye will obey my voice, and keep my covenant, then ye shall be a peculiar treasure unto me above all people" (v.5). The people, ignorant of their own ability and also of the nature of the claims of a holy God, at once accepted the terms and said, "All that the Lord hath spoken we will do."

It is well known that man totally failed to keep the law. Its unambiguous terms made no allowance for the sinner, and James 2:10 states the guilt of those who offend even in one point. The law and its claims only showed man's failure and brought condemnation upon him as a transgressor. Without going further into that matter, important though it is, we will rather notice what Scripture says about the believer's relation to divine law, before and after his conversion.

There is an important distinction to be made between "law" as a principle of God's dealings with man, and *"the* law" as given by Moses to Israel at Sinai. There is also a marked contrast between the age (or dispensation) of law, and the age (or dispensation) of grace. First of all notice that law characterises all God's dealings, in all ages. He is a God of order and of rule - in all departments of His kingdom. Heaven and earth, Israel and the Church, saints and angels, are each and all subjects of His rule. Three times to the proud Gentile king, Nebuchadnezzar, did God, through Daniel's lips, repeat the words, "The Most High ruleth in the kingdom of men, and giveth it to whomsoever He will" (Dan 4:17,25,32), and this principle is the same through all dispensations.

"The law", however, was given at a specified time, to a special people, and for a definite purpose. There was no such law from Adam to Moses (see Rom 5:13-14). The period of the law is clearly stated: "The law was given by Moses" (John 1:17); "Till the Seed should come, to whom the promise was made" (Gal 3:19). Then "grace and truth came by Jesus Christ", and "under grace", God's dealings with man continue up to this time.

The law was not given for man's salvation. "It was added because of transgression" (Gal 3:19). "The law entered that the offence might abound" (Rom 5:20). "The law is holy, just and good", but man is a sinner, and when the law reveals to man what God requires of him, he is made to know that "sin is exceeding sinful" (Rom 7:13). The whole world, convicted and tested, stands with closed mouth, "guilty before God" (see Rom 3:19; 5:12). How strange, that what God gave to show man his ruin and condemnation, should be thought of and used by many as a ladder to reach heaven by works! Yet such is man's perversity. If God gives him a law, he will promise to keep it, and yet he will openly and knowingly break its first three commandments, before it reaches him on tables of stone (see Exod 20:3-5, with Exod 32:1-5). Then if God proclaims salvation by grace (Titus

2:11), man will seek to gain that salvation by keeping fragments of a broken law (Luke 18:11-12).

To the believer, the law with its demands, holds no terror. He knows that in Christ its claims have all been met for him: "What the law could not do in that it was weak through the flesh, God sending His own Son in the likeness of sinful flesh, and for sin, condemned sin in the flesh" (Rom 8:3); "Christ is the end of the law for righteousness to every one that believeth" (Rom 10:4). In Christ the believer is judicially dead to the law: it has no further claim upon him. He is able to look it full in the face, and say, "I through the law am dead to the law, that I might live unto God" (Gal 2:19); "I have been (am) crucified with Christ" (Gal 2:20). The law cannot apprehend or condemn a dead man; and the believer has become "dead to the law through the body of Christ" (Rom 7:4). His standing is now in a risen Christ, possessing a new life, united to a new husband, controlled by a new power. "The law of the Spirit of life in Christ Jesus hath made me free from the law of sin and death" (Rom 8:2) is the language and experience of his soul.

But, it has been said, the law is the believer's "rule of life". This was what the Galatians were seeking to make it. They had begun with grace, but had then returned to the law as a "rule of life". "Ye are not under the law but under grace" (Rom 6:14) is God's answer to this. The believer is a child in the Father's house (Luke 15:32; 1 John 3:1), a subject of its rule. He is in the kingdom of God's dear Son (Col 1:13); he confesses and acknowledges Jesus as His Lord (1 Cor 12:3; Phil 3:8), and all this brings with it responsibility. But his obedience is prompted by love! His subjection is not in the spirit of a slave, but of a son. He serves in the liberty of one who has access and welcome to the innermost circle of Divine favour and love.

The believer is not a lawless person. Neither is he a legalist - he walks and serves in "the liberty wherewith Christ made him free" (Gal 5:1). All he or she does is not done out of a sense of duty or from fear of punishment; rather out of devotion of heart and mind to the One who is their Saviour and Lord. This honour belongs to all the saints. See then that you do not let it slip, dear fellow-believer, or lose it by worldliness, or in the mists of human tradition. Let Christ be the centre of your attention. Set Him before you as your example. Honour Him only as your Lord. Let His Word alone be your rule and guide for life. In this way the righteousness of the law will be fulfilled in us "who walk not after the flesh, but after the Spirit" (Rom 8:4). As you have love for Christ and for others you find that "love is the fulfilling of the law" (Rom 13:10).

CHAPTER 19

The Golden Calf

At the call of Jehovah, Moses had gone up to the Mount of God (Exod 24:13), while Aaron, Hur, and all the people were left in the valley below Mount Sinai. There they were going to be tried, their dependence and obedience tested, during the personal absence of their leader. The sequel shows how sadly they failed, and how their failure came about.

Moses was out of sight: he was in the presence of God. For a short period all seems to have gone well, but their faith and patience eventually gave way. When they saw that Moses "delayed to come down", they gathered around Aaron, and demanded that he should make for them "gods to go before" them. Coupled with this demand, they added words which at once reveal their fallen condition - "for this Moses, *the man* that brought us up out of Egypt, we wot not what is become of him". On the Red Sea shore, they had ascribed to Jehovah the glory of their deliverance and salvation (Exod 15:13); but here, under the crest of Sinai, and in sight of the glory of the Lord, like devouring fire on the mountain, they give His glory to another.

Such is man - not only by nature fallen and lost, but even after redemption and separation from the world are known, man's evil heart, dominated by unbelief, will lead him away "from the living God" (Heb 3:12). Israel "forgot God their Saviour" (Psa 106:21), and "in their hearts turned back again into Egypt" (Acts 7:39). This was the root of their sin. Aaron, wishing to please the people, and doubtless in the same condition of unbelief as themselves, invited them to take off their jewellery, and with his own hand he made from it a golden calf, which he set up before their eyes, and built an altar before it, proclaiming "a feast to the Lord". This was terrible wickedness - all the greater because it was perpetrated by a man of Aaron's standing. The crowning act of all was the association of Jehovah's holy Name with this dark idolatry.

This scene before Mount Sinai has been repeated again and again in the history of Christendom. The Lord Jesus has gone up into the immediate presence of God in heaven. His people, His church which bears His Name and calls Him Lord, is left on earth, in the place of dependence and obedience, to keep His Word, to bear testimony to His Name, and to own His Lordship, until the time of His return. "To serve" and "to wait" (1 Thess 1:9-10) was the employment and the attitude of saints of early times, but this did not continue for very long. "The hope" became obscured; the minding of "earthly things" (Phil 3:19) usurped its place. "My Lord delayeth His coming" became the language of many, and then the traditions of men, the fashion of the world, clerisy, priestcraft, and doctrines of demons, rolled in like a flood. The molten calf - the worship of Egypt, or what men now call "Natural Religion", something to appeal to men's senses and fill their eyes, took the place of "Jesus in the midst". The voices of leaders, the creeds and liturgies of men, replaced the Word of God, and the place of Christ as Son and Lord over God's house (Heb 3:6) was filled with something else.

What calls itself "The Church" to-day is so like this. It is a defiled camp where man's will and man's word rule supreme. The people, ever "set on mischief" (Exod 32:22), can always find some in high places, such as Aaron, who ought to know better, but fearing the people more than God will carry out their desires, and thus the apostasy of Christendom has been accomplished. What a sight before high heaven, that host of people at early morning offering their burnt-offerings and their peace-offerings (notably no sin-offering) before their calf, and immediately afterwards filling up their busy day in wanton revelry! "They sat down to eat and to drink, and rose up to play." Such is the world and its religion: a combination of hypocrisy and sinfulness: from the sacrament to the ballroom; from the church to the theatre; from sermons and songs to gambling and drinking. And the darkest blot, the deepest insult to a holy God is this, that men like Aaron, who had heard the counsel of heaven, and was a co-worker with Moses "the man of God", are ringleaders in this terrible shame.

While this revelry was going on in the valley, let us see what was happening on the mountain. Moses was receiving from Jehovah His very thoughts and commandments about it. So when Moses came down from the mount, he knew full well the mind of God about that shameful sight. He could not be dazzled by the excuses and lies of his brother. He had heard from Jehovah's lips that the people "had corrupted themselves"; he viewed the scene from the presence of the Lord; he looked upon it from the mount of God. This makes all the difference. A carnal man can only see sin as it affects himself or others. A spiritual man must look upon it as it dishonours God, and deal with it and those who are guilty of it, or associated with it, accordingly. When Moses had met his brother Aaron at the mount of God, a number of years before, he "kissed him" (Exod 4:27). They had both come forth from the presence of God then, their fellowship then was in the light, their love was the love of brethren. But Aaron had here lost that fellowship with God; he had gone out of the way, and led others after him. The time now was not the time to kiss, or to speak of brotherly love, and Moses knew it. Therefore he does not act as if nothing had happened, but charges home the sin of Aaron upon him. He then takes the idol which Aaron had made, burns it and grinds it to powder. This was acting according to the mind of God; it was giving effect to the judgement of heaven. Less than this would not have been appropriate. The honour of Jehovah had been trampled on, and Moses did not allow his "brotherly love" to hinder him from faithfully vindicating it.

Nor was this all. He knew that the camp could not now be the place of Jehovah's rest, so he stood in the gate and said, "Who is on the Lord's side let him come unto me?" It was not a question now of who were Israelites - that had been made clear on the night of their exodus from Egypt. But now it was - "Who is *for* Jehovah?" "And all the sons of Levi gathered themselves together unto him." They took their place on Jehovah's side, openly and definitely, and for this they received the Lord's approval, and His "covenant of life and peace" (see Deut 33:8-9 ; Mal 2:5). They did not shun to execute the judgement of the Lord, even upon their brethren, for the fear of the Lord and the honour of His Name was primarily before them.

In this day of a defiled camp, an apostate church, in which the name of God is dishonoured, the Lordship of Christ ignored, and His Word regarded as unimportant, the call is again heard - Who is on the Lord's side? It is not a question of who are Christians, but of who are willing to give the Lord His place and take their stand with Him. To do this, many may have to leave their dearest earthly treasures, in order to obey the will of God, and remove themselves from associations where He has been dishonoured. This may cut many a link, and break many a lifelong friendship. It will be sure to cost us something, perhaps more than flesh and blood can bear, but to those who set the Lord before them, and by grace determine to be on His side, strength will be given to go forth "without the camp", and to use "the sword of the Spirit, which is the Word of God", to accomplish whatever He has commanded.

"And Moses took the Tabernacle and pitched it without the camp, and called it the Tabernacle of the congregation", or the "Tent of appointed meeting". "And it came to pass that every one which sought the Lord, went out unto the Tabernacle of the congregation (Tent of appointed meeting) which was without the camp" (Exod 33:7). And thus it is, that all who seek the Lord, and hear the call of a rejected Christ, whose name and claims have been dishonoured in what professes to be the church, "go forth unto *Him* without the camp" (Heb 13:13), gathering unto His Name alone, to hear His voice as the one Shepherd of His flock, to own His claims over them individually as His disciples, and His authority and rule in "the house of God, the church of the living God, the pillar and ground of the truth" (1 Tim 3:14-15).

CHAPTER 20

Jehovah's Dwelling Place

The tabernacle which the Lord asked His redeemed people to build for Him was His dwelling place in their midst. Its fabric was composed of materials brought by the freewill offerings of the people (Exod 25:1-2; 36:3), and built according to the divine pattern, shown to Moses on the mount (Exod 25:8-9; 39:32). There the pillar of cloud - the manifested presence of Jehovah - came down and filled the sanctuary. It visible upon it, by day and by night. The twelve tribes encamped around it, in a divinely ordered fashion. Here it was that sacrifice and priesthood, divine worship and service, were carried through day after day.

There was no sanctuary in Egypt. Redemption and separation had to be experienced before there could be a dwelling place for God, or a place of worship and service for man. The tabernacle was a shadow of good things to come. It pointed onward to Christ. Its sacrifices were foreshadowings of the one perfect Sacrifice. Its priesthood was typical of the present priesthood of Christ in heaven. Of course there are many points of contrast, for the law "was not the very image" of the things foreshadowed. For example, the sacrifices were imperfect, and had then to be repeated year after year. The priesthood passed from generation to generation - priests came and went. But "Christ being come" (Heb 9:11-14), we have in Him a perfect sacrifice, of eternal value, and a Priest who abides and lives for ever. We will not go into more details of these tabernacle types here as we have in another book*.

The tabernacle was the divine centre around which the

*See *The Tabernacle in the Wilderness* by John Ritchie.

chosen people gathered, each in his divinely-ordered place. Divine rule was acknowledged there: His commandments were obeyed in all matters concerning His glory, and His people's welfare. From the door of that tabernacle He spoke and gave commandments concerning all that pertained to His worship and the order of His house (see Lev 1:1), and of all that belonged to the people in their service, their work, and their warfare (see Num 1:1).

The tabernacle and the camp - "the church in the wilderness" (Acts 7:38), the place of the divine dwelling, and the circle of divine rule, is typical of the church of God, His dwelling place, and His kingdom. There, in the midst of the nations, separated from all and not reckoned as worthy of a place among them, were the people of Jehovah, His peculiar treasure, "a people near unto Him" (Psa 148:14). He dwelt in their midst, and among them He ruled as their King (Num 23:21). This was the distinctive glory of Israel, and their power among their enemies. Yet they sinned it all away, and demanded a king to be like the nations around them (1 Sam 8:6), and in the reckoning of God they thus rejected Him (1 Sam 8:19). For God's people today to elect a leader, to make choice of one man as their minister, is virtually to thrust the Lord Jesus from His place "in the midst" (Matt 18:20) of His people. The man may have many gifts; he may stand head and shoulders above all around him, like Saul, the man of the people's choice, but that makes no difference. In principle, God is rejected, and the Lordship of Christ is disowned. May God's saints learn that clerisy and human rule is not God's will or way for His people in the church today, and simply gather around and cleave to Christ, as their only Lord and centre, "in the midst".

CHAPTER 21

The Mission of the Spies

At first sight it may appear as if the sending forth of the twelve spies to search the land of Canaan had its origin in the commandment of the Lord, but by comparing Deut 1:22 with Num 13:1-3, it is clear that it originated in the will of man: "Ye came near unto me, every one of you, and said, We will send men before us, and they shall search out the land." And when we remember what the object of the mission was, it only confirms the fact that it was the fruit of unbelief and disregard of the Word of God. He gave them their desire, as He afterwards did when they desired a king, but neither the sending of the spies nor the provision of a king, was the will of God.

When the purpose of Jehovah for the deliverance of His people from Egypt was first made known to Moses, and through him to the people, it was in the glowing words, "I am come down to deliver them out of the hand of the Egyptians, and to bring them out of that land, unto a good land and a large, unto a land flowing with milk and honey" (Exod 3:8). They had already had the first and second parts of this definite promise fulfilled to them. They had been delivered from the Egyptians, and brought up out of their land. They might have well counted on their faithful God to fulfil what remained, and gone forward counting on Him to do it. But instead of trusting God, and believing His Word, they demanded that spies be sent to "see the land what it is", whether it be "good or bad", whether it be "fat or lean" (Num 13:18-20). This was equivalent to saying, "We cannot accept God's description of the land of Canaan, we must have it confirmed by man." True, He told us that the land is "good", but we will send to see whether it be "good or bad". He said it was "flowing with milk and honey", but we must see whether it be "fat or lean".

With this spirit prevailing, it is easy to account for the attitude of the whole congregation when the spies returned bringing back their "evil report". They were ready to receive the report of unbelieving men, to give it full credit, and to disbelieve God. This is the way of man's heart. The spies when they returned were unable to say anything against the land. The testimony wrung from them was that it flowed with "milk and honey", but that was immediately followed by an prolonged description of the enemies and obstacles they would have to meet in taking possession of it. They saw walled cities and great giants there, and themselves "as grasshoppers". Not a word was said about God and His promise at all. God was out of their reckoning. His promise, "I will bring you in," had no place in their hearts. "They could not enter in because of unbelief." "They said one to another, let us make a captain and return to Egypt" (Num 14:4). In their hearts they were there already (see 11:5), and where the heart is, the feet will soon follow. They stood at Kadesh-barnea - on the very borders of the goodly land. Its fruits lay before them. They were reminded that the Lord was able to bring them in and give it to them, and yet in the face of all this, they turned their backs upon it, and refused to enter in.

This marked a crisis in their history. Jehovah had patiently borne with them in their murmurings and all their failures in the wilderness, but now He must judge and punish this deliberate rejection of the inheritance, this bold declaration of their unbelief of His Word. Had it not been for the intercession of Moses on their behalf, the righteous wrath of an offended God would have destroyed them in a moment. The unbelieving people, however, were held to their choice. They must now tramp on through the wilderness for forty long years. There they must all die and be buried. Their children would enter and possess the land, but those who despised it must perish before they get there.

There are solemn lessons here for the children of God. That goodly land of promise is the type of the vast inheritance of spiritual blessings (Eph 1:3) to which every believer in Christ has access and title. But these must be entered into in order to be possessed. It is not what the eye takes in, but what the foot covers, that is possessed. Acquaintance with the geography of a country is one thing; to stand on its soil is quite another. And so there may be theoretical knowledge of heavenly things, with little or no possession of them in the soul. To take possession of spiritual blessings is sure to bring us into the place of "the sons of Anak", and the "walled cities". "Grapes" and "giants" are usually found together, and if we would feed on the one, we must fight the other. This is just where many fail. They would have the blessings, but they fear the fight. The "grapes" are sweet, but the "giants" are strong; and rather than get to grips with them, they despise the whole inheritance of spiritual blessing, and go back to worldliness and backsliding.

How often have we seen Christians on the very borders of the heavenly Canaan, enamoured it may be with the blessedness of a life of faith, of an out-and-out discipleship and obedience to the Word of the Lord! But then the cross has to be borne. Friends will oppose; the world will revile; it may be there will be loss of earthly things. These are the "walled cities" and the "giants", by which the faith of many is tested. They did not count on these, although, had they read their Bibles, they might have known, that their Lord had said, "If any man will come after Me, let him deny himself, and take up his cross daily, and follow Me" (Luke 9:23). And so they turn again to the world in some of its many forms, and there continue and end their days, unhappy backsliders, stumbling blocks to others, and eternal losers to themselves. The further history of this unbelieving people is a blank: God does not consider it worthwhile to write it. From the time that they "despised the pleasant land", until they returned to its borders after thirty-eight weary years of wandering, there is nothing recorded in these books of Scripture, except the stoning of the Sabbath breaker, and the sin and doom of Korah and his company. These acts have a striking significance in the history of this fallen and rebellious people, and they undoubtedly have their anti-types in the backslidings and apostacies of many in Christendom (see Heb 10:28; Jude 11).

It is a relief now to turn away from these unbelievers to the two faithful men who stood out and boldly confessed their faith in the living God. Caleb and Joshua were two of the twelve men chosen to spy out the land, but they were of "another spirit" from the rest. They believed God. They counted Him faithful who had promised. They were men prepared to follow the Lord "fully" (Num 14:24). As Caleb confessed, when he stood in the land of Canaan, forty-five years later, "I brought him word again as it was in mine heart" (Josh 14:7). Even if Caleb had been led through the land of Canaan blindfolded, he would have said it was "a good land" all the same. He did not gain his information from what he saw, but from what the Lord his God had said. The Word of the Lord was in his heart. He believed God, both as regards the land, and His power to bring them into it. He saw the walled cities, he saw the giants, but above all these, greater than them all, he saw the living God. He believed that God was "well able" to give them the victory, and he testified, "Let us go up at once and possess it, for we are well able to overcome it." This was not the language of pride or self-sufficiency : it was the language of faith. This is apparent from the words with which he backed up his exhortation, "And the Lord is with us, fear them not" (Num 14:9). What a blessed testimony! And although it had no effect on the unbelieving people, it was duly valued and rewarded by the God of heaven.

When the ten unbelieving spies lay dead in the wilderness, Caleb and Joshua lived still (Num 14:36-38). And they received the promise of Jehovah that He would bring them into the land which their brethren had despised. They had to wait forty long years for the fulfilment of the promise - and thus they add to their faith patience. They had to tread the wilderness side by side with those who would have stoned them, and see one after another fall by their side, but they knew that God's promise could not fail. How blessed to read the sequel to all this as recorded in Joshua 14:6-15: to see these old warriors in the land flowing with milk and honey, and to hear from Caleb's lips his thrilling testimony to the faithfulness of God. There he stood, hale and hearty, at the age of eighty-five, strong, and able for war as in the days of his youth, ready to go up and take possession of his inheritance, still counting on the Lord to drive out the enemy. Hebron - which means "fellowship" - became his inheritance, and from it he drove out the three sons of Anak, who had terrified the whole host of Israel.

From this episode in the wilderness we can learn the valuable lesson that God is ever faithful to those who trust Him, and that the path of blessing and of fellowship with God is the path of faithfulness and obedience to all that the Lord has commanded in His Word.

"He always wins who sides with God; to him no chance is lost;
God's will is sweetest to him, when it triumphs at his cost."

CHAPTER 22

Nearing the End of the Journey

The closing chapters of the book of Numbers record the final events of the wilderness journey. They also are full of instruction and solemn warning to us in these last days, and we can briefly examine them now.

The death of Miriam (Num 20:1)

The sweet singer who had led the song of praise on the Red Sea shore passes off the scene through death, and is buried in the wilderness of Kadesh. Like many a young believer, she made a bright and promising start of the pilgrim pathway, but her sky soon became overcast with clouds of doubt. She shared the murmurings and the unbelief of the rest of the people, and for this she must die along with the others in the wilderness. From this we may surely learn a solemn lesson. It is good to begin our christian life with a song, but if we wish to end our pilgrim days in praise, and have an abundant entrance into the kingdom, we must keep going on with God all the time.

The sin of Moses (Num 20:7-11)

Of all the failures and sins of the wilderness, the failure of Moses, the man of God, is one of the saddest, and carries most solemn instruction to the people of God. He was commanded to take the rod, and "speak to the rock" that its streams of refreshing water might flow towards the thirsty people who were complaining once again. But Moses in anger struck the rock with his rod, and instead spoke to the people. He spoke "unadvisedly with his lips", and for this he was prevented from entering the land of promise. True, the people "provoked his spirit" (Psa 106:33), but this did not lessen his sin in the eyes of a holy God, his disobedience to the Lord's command. His high position, his former faithfulness, his nearness to God, and his personal meekness, did not compensate for his sin and this grievous dishonour to Jehovah. Neither his earnest pleadings with God, nor his longing desire to enter the land (Deut 3:25-27), could alter the word of the Lord.

There are solemn lessons for our souls here. Disobedience, even in a saint, can never go unpunished. True, there is "no condemnation to them that are in Christ Jesus" (Rom 8:1), but there is the discipline and chastisement from a loving heavenly Father, such as the world knows nothing of (Heb 12:6). A child of God can never lose his place in the divine family, but if he sins wilfully he must receive the discipline of a Father's hand. The higher his place, the greater his privilege, then the more severe his chastisement will be. Thus it was with Moses. He was permitted to see the goodly land, from the heights of mount Nebo, and to end his life on earth with undimmed eye. He was honoured as no man was ever honoured before, nor has been since, in being buried by the very hand of God. But he was not allowed to lead the ransomed people whom he loved and had served so well, into their inheritance. As the representative of the law he could not this in any case; but as the servant of God, he failed through disobedience, and was prohibited.

The death of Aaron (Num 20:23-29)

Aaron the high priest was the next to pass away. He was led up to the top of mount Hor, and there stripped of his official robes, and gathered unto his people. He is the representative of that order of priesthood which was of the law, and he stands in contrast to Christ, whose priesthood shall never finish or pass to another. "Thou art a priest *for ever,* after the order of Melchisedec" (Heb 7:21), is the divine decree to Christ. Because of this we may always draw near to God in prayer and worship, and to His throne of grace for help in every time of need (Heb 4:14-16).

Balaam and Balak (Num 22 - 24)

As the wilderness journey drew near to its close, another enemy advanced to meet this pilgrim people. This was Balak, the king of Moab, assisted by Balaam, the covetous prophet. We cannot go into all the details of this extraordinary collaboration, or trace all the devices of this accomplished servant of Satan. Suffice to say that his objective was to curse the people of God, and to exterminate those whom Jehovah had chosen and redeemed.

The time he selected for this was at the end of their wanderings through the wilderness, after forty long years of provocation and unfaithfulness to God. Balaam thought that he would easily incite Jehovah to curse the people because of their long continued failures. But in this he was mistaken. Instead of pronouncing his curse, his mouth was filled with blessings which God gave him to speak. Instead of a solemn indictment against God's people, Balaam poured forth, in grand and lofty language such as He had never used before, a description of God's delight in His redeemed people, their glorious standing in His grace, their present calling, and their glory to come.

This is so like our blessed Lord. He will reprove and chastise His people for their disobedience Himself, but He will not allow an enemy to raise his voice against them. He will not listen to the adversary as their accuser. Satan may seek cause against the saints, but he cannot obtain judgement against them. "It is God that justifieth, who is he that condemneth?" (Rom 8:33-34). In the presence of God, Satan may accuse us, but he cannot condemn us, and the day will come, when he shall be cast down from his place, as the "accuser of the brethren", finally to be trampled under the feet of the saints, who are overcomers "by the blood of the Lamb" (Rom 16:20; Rev 12:10-11). Praise the Lord!

But another strategy of the enemy had yet to be revealed. If he cannot destroy the people of the Lord by cursing, he will try to seduce them by craftiness and deceit. When the devil fails to overcome the saints as "the roaring lion", he often seeks to seduce them as "the subtle serpent", and alas, this wile of his too often succeeds. Scripture states concerning this second device of Balaam, that "he taught Balak to cast a stumbling-block before the children of Israel" (Rev 2:14), and by this he succeeded in joining the chosen and separated people of God with those who are unclean. The reference to this in New Testament times as "the doctrine of Balaam", in the church at Thyatira, warns us that the same tactic will be used to drag the church of God into unholy alliances with the world. And has it not succeeded? Full well the devil knows that a corrupted church, intermingled with the ungodly, unequally yoked with unbelievers, will be spoiled for God and have no effective testimony for Him in the world. Let the saints of God be fully awake to this. Already there are many anti-Christs: "the mystery of iniquity doth already work". A chief part of Satan's business among the saints is to seduce them into alliance and spiritual whoredom with the world, and thus blot out their testimony as a redeemed and separated people unto the Lord.

The wilderness inheritance (Num 32)

Two and a half tribes out of the twelve want to obtain their inheritance on the wilderness side of the river Jordan, outside the land of promise. This represents another form of borderland Christianity all too common in our day. They were attracted by the land of Gilead and its good pastureland, as a place for their cattle. Self and self-interest guided them in their choice, as it had guided Lot in earlier times (see Gen 13:10), and for this they choose to part company with their brethren, and to forfeit their share of the promised land. They did maintain a kind of unity with them, after their own design (see Joshua 22:10), but they were always a source of weakness and trouble to those who did go in and dwell in the land.

This generation is still to be found among the people of the Lord. The Lord's name is named by them: they claim to be the people of God, but the place of their dwelling, and the manner of their life and testimony, savours more of earth than of heaven. They profess to be part of the "heavenly calling", yet it is evident that "earthly things" are closer to their hearts than "the things which are above". The "better part" is that land across the Jordan, in that country where the eye of the God of Israel rests continually, and where He dwells in His tabernacle in the midst of His people. May that be the place we seek to live in, close to the Lord and in fellowship with His dear people.

CHAPTER 23

On the Borders of Canaan

The final stage of the long wilderness journey has been reached at long last, and the pilgrim people come within sight of the land of promise. Canaan, the place of their inheritance, spreads itself out before them in all its richness and beauty. The land flowing with milk and honey, the brooks of water, the fountains that spring out of valleys and hills, the wealthy cornfields and vineyards, the beautiful plains, all as the Lord had described them, are now in full view. How that glorious sight must have stirred their hearts. Only one thing now remained to do: that was to "arise and possess the land".

It was all theirs already by promise, but they must now tread on it in order to possess it. The word of Jehovah was, "Every place that the sole of your foot shall tread upon, that have I given you." It was not enough to behold it, or even to be able to describe it - they must plant their feet upon its soil in order to possess and enjoy it. The measure of their actual possession was that which they covered with their foot, no more. We may learn an important lesson here. In spiritual things it is not what we know, but what we actually possess that enriches our souls. Theoretical knowledge, apart from appropriating faith, is of little value. To read the words in the Book of God, "Blessed with all spiritual blessings" is one thing; to have these blessings as a matter of realisation in the soul is another and far more important. The measure of our actual spiritual wealth is not what we see contained in the promises of God in Scripture, but what we ourselves get out of them from day to day. "All spiritual blessings" are ours in Christ, but the measure in which they will be in *us,* will be limited by our faith's foothold on them.

When the people moved from Shittim, their last camping-place in the wilderness, and came to the banks of the Jordan, it was harvest time, the season of the earth's richest blessing. They saw the land of their possession at its very best. But a barrier lay between them and that goodly land. The river Jordan - "the Descender", deep and wide, overflowing its banks, impeded their progress. What were they to do? *Go forward,* and leave God to deal with the difficulty. They had proved His faithfulness already in dividing the waters of the Red Sea for them to pass through when they came out of Egypt, and the same Lord God was with them and for them now, on the banks of the river Jordan.

We must clarify the meaning of the river Jordan, the type before us now. Many people regard the river Jordan to mean death, and Canaan, lying beyond it, to be the type of heaven. In many of our hymns, "crossing the Jordan" is generally supposed to mean the believer's death, and the "shining shore" and "lovely landscape" on the other side, to be the place to which the ransomed spirit of the Christian goes, when it leaves the mortal body. It is certainly true that when a believer in Christ dies, he or she goes to be with Christ, which is far better than the best on earth, and language fails to describe adequately the bliss and glory of heaven. But this is not what the type here before us is designed to teach. "The other side of Jordan" cannot mean that heaven to which the believer goes, when earthly life is past. In heaven there are no difficult walled cities, no giants, no chariots of iron to fear. The believer does not there handle the sword and shield, does not fight with enemies, does not wear the warrior's armour. He rests with Christ. He is in Paradise. His fight is fought, his warfare is ended (2 Tim 4:7-8). But when Israel crossed the Jordan, and entered Canaan, they really had to fight. They entered as "men of war" to handle sword and shield. Enemies were active there to contest their right to possess the land. God had said, "Thou shalt smite them and utterly destroy them" (Deut 7:2).

Canaan here is rather the type of the believer's present place of blessing, as we have it expressed in the glowing words: "Blessed be the God and Father of our Lord Jesus Christ, who *hath* blessed us with spiritual blessings in *heavenly* places in Christ" (Eph 1:3). Here is our spiritual Canaan, our "land flowing with milk and honey". It is noteworthy that in the same Epistle (Ephesians), we have also our enemies and our warfare described. "We wrestle not against flesh and blood, but against principalities, against powers, against the rulers of the darkness of this world, against spiritual wickedness (or wicked spirits), in heavenly places" (Eph 6:12, margin). Here we have our "Canaanites", seeking to force us from our ground, oppose us in our progress, and hinder us from possessing our blessings now. But as we read on we find that "the whole armour of God" has been provided for us to wear - take it up and put it on! It will enable the christian warrior to meet the enemy, and under his divine Joshua, his glorious Leader, the Captain of Salvation, the risen Christ, to take possession of this goodly land of promise.

CHAPTER 24

Crossing Jordan

The long looked for day at last arrived, and the command of the Lord was, "Arise, go over this Jordan" (Josh 1:2). The impetuous river, overflowing its banks, stretched itself out before them, barring their access to the goodly land. But Jordan's swelling tide must yield to the power of "the Lord of all the earth", who is now leading His people forward to the place of their inheritance.

The rod of Moses had been used as the instrument to divide the Red Sea forty years before this, but that rod, and the hand that held it, are not present here at Jordan. "The ark of the covenant", with its mercy-seat and covering of blue, carried on the shoulders of the Levites clothed in their priestly garments, is now to be the instrument of Israel's deliverance. As soon as the priests carrying the sacred ark, dipped their feet in the brim of the swelling river, its waters were cut off. Jordan's flood rolled back - and rose up in a heap, away back by the city Adam (a place unknown, but the significance of its name, in connection with the first man, and the death brought on by him, is evident). The waters cut off rolled on, flowing into the Dead Sea, to be seen no more. There was literally no Jordan visible to Israel that day. The dry bed of the river stretched as far as the eye could see on either side. The priests with the ark on their shoulders, stood between the people and the heaped-up waters, so they "hasted and passed over". So long as the priests, with the ark of the covenant, stood there between the people and the heaped-up waters, not a drop could reach them. Before the weakest child in Israel could be touched by these waters, they would have to overwhelm the priests and the ark. So long as the feet of the priests "stood firm" in Jordan's bed, the people were absolutely safe, as safe as Jehovah could make them. And thus the whole host, men of war, old men and women and little children alike, passed "clean over" Jordan, in the full light of day, and placed their feet on their inheritance on the Canaan side of the river.

This inspiring sight has more typical lessons for the children of God. Looking back we see that the paschal Lamb and the sprinkled blood in Egypt pointed onward to the death of Christ, as that which saves us from the wages of sin and from the wrath to come. Then the Red Sea tells of deliverance from Satan's power, and separation from the world, by the cross of Christ. Now Jordan is a type of Christ's death and resurrection, as that by which death is abolished, judgement passed away, and a way opened into heaven for the people of God. Israel's passage through the dried-up river bed tells of the believer experimentally and practically taking possession of this great truth in his soul, and reckoning himself dead, buried, and risen with Christ. To grasp these glorious truths by faith, to make them one's own, is the entrance to a wide and wealthy range of spiritual blessing. In that goodly land are "all spiritual blessings in heavenly places", "the unsearchable riches of Christ", "the exceeding riches of His grace", "the exceeding greatness of His power" - these are things known and enjoyed by the believer now in that land which lies "beyond Jordan". The person who lives as a man in the flesh or a man of the world may read about them, and even speak about them, but the enjoyment of them is known only by the one who reckons himself dead and risen with Christ.

CHAPTER 25

Memorials of Jordan at Gilgal

The miraculous passage of Israel across the river Jordan was not to be forgotten. So twelve chosen men, one from each tribe, are now told to return to the emptied bed of the river, to the place where the priests' feet were still standing, and from there each is to lift a stone. These twelve stones will be carried on their shoulders to the Canaan side of the river, and set up on the promised land in a place called Gilgal (Josh 4:19). These stones were to be memorials of the Lord's power in cutting off the waters of Jordan, and in bringing His people into the land. They were to be witnesses to future generations of the power of the Lord's right hand.

These memorial stones were raised up from the place of death and carried by a power outside themselves to a new position, in which they were to bear witness for God. They remind us of the present place of those who are risen and seated with Christ. Like these stones, once they lay in death, under judgement, but now by the grace and power of God, they have been raised up and seated together in heavenly places in Christ. Believers living in this position, and manifesting by a daily life for God that their affection is set on things above, will soon attract the world's attention. The question will be asked, "What mean ye by these stones?" Gilgal - where Israel's reproach was rolled away - was a continual witness to "all the people of the earth" of what the hand of the Lord had wrought for His people Israel (Josh 4:24).

Another memorial had also to be set up in a different place.

In the deep bed of Jordan, in the place where the priests' feet stood, Joshua set up twelve more stones, to be overflowed and buried by the waters of Jordan when they returned in their strength. Here we have the other side of the picture, the balancing truth we might say. The twelve stones lifted out of Jordan, and set up in Canaan's land, tell of the new standing of the believer, as risen with Christ. The twelve stones buried in Jordan, never more to be seen by human eyes, tell of the believer's death and burial with Christ.

Baptism is the New Testament answer to the two sets of memorial stones in and beyond Jordan. It is the divinely appointed figure of the believer's death, burial, and resurrection with Christ (Rom 6:3-4). To those who have been baptised, and by faith appropriate and experience the reality of the meaning of baptism, the likeness to these memorial stones will be clear and precious.

The Book of Joshua goes on to tell of the conquest of the land of Canaan, and the distribution of the inheritance among the tribes of Israel. The energy, zeal, and faith displayed by the people, the conquests and victories won by them, the enemies conquered, and also the mistakes made, are all full of instruction for us. In this our day there is so much easy going indifference in spiritual things that we need to be stirred up to earnest endeavour and seriousness in the things of God. May it be ours, in the same spirit of faith, to press on in the battle, wearing the whole armour of the Lord, enduring hardness as "good soldiers of Jesus Christ".